T0358420

# ROUTLEDGE LIBRARY EDITIONS: PUBLIC ENTERPRISE AND PRIVATIZATION

Volume 6

# PUBLIC ENTERPRISE IN BRITAIN

# PUBLIC ENTERPRISE IN BRITAIN

Thoughts on Recent Experiences

V.V. RAMANADHAM

Routledge
Taylor & Francis Group

LONDON AND NEW YORK

First published in 1959 by Frank Cass & Company Ltd

This edition first published in 2019
by Routledge
2 Park Square, Milton Park, Abingdon, Oxon OX14 4RN

and by Routledge
52 Vanderbilt Avenue, New York, NY 10017

*Routledge is an imprint of the Taylor & Francis Group, an informa business*

*British Library Cataloguing in Publication Data*
A catalogue record for this book is available from the British Library

ISBN: 978-0-367-14233-9 (Set)
ISBN: 978-0-429-25929-6 (Set) (ebk)
ISBN: 978-0-367-19122-1 (Volume 6) (hbk)
ISBN: 978-0-429-20059-5 (Volume 6) (ebk)

**Publisher's Note**
The publisher has gone to great lengths to ensure the quality of this reprint but points out that some imperfections in the original copies may be apparent.

**Disclaimer**
The publisher has made every effort to trace copyright holders and would welcome correspondence from those they have been unable to trace.

# PUBLIC ENTERPRISE
## IN
# BRITAIN

Thoughts on Recent Experiences

### V. V. RAMANADHAM

M.Com. (Hons.), Ph.D. (Andhra)
Ph.D. (Lond.), Assoc. Inst. T.
Formerly Nuffield Fellow
London School of Economics

FRANK CASS & COMPANY LTD
LONDON
1959

PRINTED IN GREAT BRITAIN BY
EBENEZER BAYLIS AND SON, LIMITED, THE
TRINITY PRESS, WORCESTER, AND LONDON

To
CHANDRAVATI

# CONTENTS

# INTRODUCTION

THIS book does not contain an argument on whether nationalization is desirable or not. On the assumption that there is nationalization, an attempt is made to discuss certain important problems raised by it in the fields of management, pricing, resource allocation and public control. It is hoped that a discussion of this nature will contribute towards ensuring the most satisfactory results from nationalization.

In many countries nationalization will remain a permanent form of industrial organization, though its extent and the industries involved will vary from country to country. Public enterprise in Britain may be considered as an experiment, from which valuable conclusions may be drawn. Four special features of Britain's experience are outstanding. Firstly, by and large, the nationalization measures have not been prompted by glaringly doctrinal considerations. On the other hand, the recent pronouncements by the Labour Party attempt to justify each nationalization on relevant and economic grounds. Secondly, the pace of nationalization has slowed down; and there has been some denationalization as well. Though this is partly due to the change in Government since 1951, one suspects that fundamentally the country is considering afresh the desirability of the kind of nationalization undertaken between 1945 and 1951. Thirdly, the great emphasis placed in this country on economic principles in the working of the nationalized industries gives the impression that it is not the purpose of nationalization to abolish the concept of consumer's freedom, the working of the price mechanism and competitive forces in the evolution of these industries. To what extent these principles have been preserved under nationalization is another question. Fourthly, from time to time changes have been introduced in the legislation governing the nationalized industries, so as to provide for their better organization. The Electricity Act of 1957, which gives effect to certain recommendations of the Herbert Committee, is a good example. It may, therefore, be suggested that a careful study of recent British experience in the field of public enterprise has much to contribute towards the understanding of problems presented by a public sector being enlarged gradually for reasons other than those of political doctrine.

It is difficult to generalize on the problems of nationalization, since nationalization has not the same form or economic content in every case. In organization, nationalized industries may vary from being of the departmental type, to being a public corporation, a joint stock

9

company or a majority holding of shares in a company. Secondly, the extent of an industry covered by nationalization may vary from one field to another—e.g., all coal mining is nationalized in Britain, whereas a part of electricity generation remains private and outside the purview of the Central Electricity Generating Board. Thirdly, the public sector, on the whole, has been the result of nationalization of privately owned industries in Britain—except in such cases as the Atomic Energy Commission; whereas elsewhere in the world, e.g., in India, it includes equally industries which have been brought into being by the Government.

In view of the varying content and significance of nationalization from case to case and country to country, one has to be careful in discussing the question of nationalization in general terms. The British scene offers the advantage of some homogeneity, in that the recently nationalized industries have all been given the public corporation form and that nationalization has resulted mainly from the taking over of private enterprises. While most inferences of the present inquiry stem directly from and apply to the British situation, a few of them relate to nationalization of the kind not found in Britain. The latter have been included in order to get a sufficiently comprehensive grasp of the problems posed by nationalization in general.

The nature of certain problems varies from one kind of nationalization to another. For example, the problem of public accountability takes the simplest form under the departmental method, while it becomes complex under the corporation method. Likewise, there are some characteristics of managerial behaviour which are inherent in nationalization, while there are certain of them which are specific to particular kinds of organization. Chapter II, dealing with the managerial function under nationalization, illustrates this point; and one should keep it in mind while following the argument presented there.

There is a conceptual difficulty in defining a public corporation. The pre-war and the post-war corporations in this country differ in some respects. (The London Passenger Transport Board remains unique in this field, thwarting all attempts at a comprehensive definition.) Corporations differ from country to country in Board constitution, relations with Government, pricing policies and disposal of profits. It is, therefore, impossible to find a definition which covers all existing cases. Yet there are some basic characteristics underlying the majority of the corporations of which typical ones are to be found with the British public corporations. For the purposes of the present inquiry, a public corporation is defined as a nationalized industry which is not organized as a department of Government, nor run by a local authority, nor given the joint stock company form and which operates on the principle of financial self-support.

An attempt has been made in this work to present a norm towards which the public corporation as an institution in the field of industrial organization should strive if its basic objects are to be achieved most satisfactorily. Many an existing corporation deviates from the norm in some way or other. But it is well worth while to endeavour to find an ideal towards which the institution should develop.

A word about the plan of the book. Essentially it contains some thoughts on certain aspects of British public enterprise, based on recent experience. There is no attempt either to cover all aspects of nationalization or to present full studies of individual nationalized industries. I have tried to select questions of fundamental interest and, while dealing with them, have drawn on the evidence supplied by these industries. A case study of electricity pricing is presented in order to give a concrete shape to my suggestions in regard to pricing decisions in the sphere of one industry.

Another purpose I had in mind was to make, on the basis of British experience, suggestions that would be of general use in the field of public enterprise. It is from this angle that I applied myself to such questions as the most desirable status of a public corporation *vis-à-vis* the Government, the most satisfactory form of central organization for a nationalized industry and the best form of consumer organization.

Lastly, I have included, where relevant, brief discussions on points not applicable to the British situation—e.g., the place of the public corporation in an under-developed economy and the problems of the joint stock company form of public enterprise. These questions are of significance to many countries of the world; and I thought the discussion would have the advantage of showing the problems in their proper perspective, with the background of British experience.

Perhaps it is necessary for me to add that I am not unaware of the difficulties in translating into practice certain suggestions which I have made on optimum units, discrimination and cross-subsidization. Nevertheless I feel that the fullest possible attempt should be made by the nationalized industries to proceed in the direction of sound economic theory. Empirical research is bound to be of great help in this respect.

Finally, there may be mentioned a few points of interest for under-developed countries as they look at the British experience of public enterprise. The British experience is distinctive in many respects. Firstly, the public sector mainly consists of industries taken over from private hands. These were already well-developed when taken over. Several studies on the reorganization of industries like gas and electricity were available; and as going concerns these industries had well-defined methods of operation. Whatever opinion one may have on the desirability of continuing those methods, it is certain that the British have had the advantage of not having to start from scratch in the field of public enterprise. One of the great advantages that followed was that, in general, the same managers as under private enterprise were at the helm of affairs under nationalization. Here again, whatever one may think on ideological grounds, managerial continuity has prevailed and this has been of no small value. In all these respects the problems faced by the governments that have launched new industrial projects are bound to be different and perhaps call for greater skill in initial organization and in the taking of right risks. Secondly, the developing countries of the world are handicapped greatly by the dearth of managerial skill, both in quality and in quantity. Further, diverse views are held on the suitability of certain successful businessmen for appointment to the boards of nationalized industries. This may prompt the governments to find managers from within the civil service, with all the consequent problems. Lastly, the success of public enterprise depends on a proper balance between economic and political considerations; and in countries where both the industrial traditions and the traditions of political control over economic affairs are yet to be built up, the tasks of public enterprise and of Government are very difficult. It is desirable that, in assessing the British experience, the under-developed countries should give due weight to these three factors.

\* \* \*

In connection with this work I am particularly grateful to Professor Sir Arnold Plant, from whom I have had invaluable help. I am conscious of his deep influence on my analytical outlook and techniques and appreciate the many suggestions he has made during my discussions with him over the last year. I am grateful to Mr. D. N. Chester who has shown great interest in my work and generously offered his criticism after going through the draft at different stages. I thank Professor P. Sargant Florence for his very helpful comments on Chapters II, IV and VI. I received valuable suggestions from Professor R. S. Edwards, Deputy Chairman of the Electricity Council, on Chapters II and III; Professor W. A. Robson and Dr. I. M. D. Little on Chapter VI; Mr. P. Chantler, Economic Adviser to the Ministry of Power, and Mr. A. F. Schumachar, Economic Adviser to the National Coal Board, on Chapter III; Mr. H. A. Clegg on Chapters II and IV; Mr. A. H. Hanson and Mr. H. Maddick on Chapters I and V; Mr. L. Foldes on Chapters III and VI and Appendices A and B; and Mr. A. D. Knox on Chapter VI. The criticism offered by them has been of great use to me in developing my argument and I offer them my warm thanks. To Dr. N. D. Vandyk I am especially indebted for the very patient and meticulous way in which he has read the whole draft and for his many suggestions on style and presentation.

I must add that, while I benefited from my discussions with all those mentioned, I alone am responsible for the views expressed in the book.

This work has been undertaken under an Award made by the Nuffield Foundation tenable in the United Kingdom for a year. I thank the Nuffield Foundation for the Award and the Director of London School of Economics for the facilities given for my work at the School.

In conclusion I should like to thank the many others, too numerous to mention individually, whose co-operation and help have facilitated the publication of this book.

Nuffield Fellow      V. V. RAMANADHAM
London School of Economics
July 1958.

# CHAPTER I

# NATIONALIZATION AND THE PUBLIC CORPORATION

THE public corporation as an institutional form of industrial organization has come to stay. The Mersey Docks and Harbour Board, established in 1857, is often cited as its remote ancestor in Great Britain; the Tennessee Valley Authority has focused world-wide attention on it; Herbert Morrison helped to give a shape to its essentials, originally in connection with the reorganization of London Transport in the 'thirties; and in the post-war nationalization programmes of Great Britain the public corporation has been the chosen form of organization.[1] It is employed very widely in most parts of the world today.

The plan of the present discussion is as follows. At the outset the characteristics which ought to be found in a public corporation are mentioned. An attempt is then made to show the circumstances in which a public enterprise ought to be organized as a corporation. The third section deals with the rationale of governmental control over corporations. This, by implication, may be generalized as a discussion of government control over the commercial enterprises in the public sector, which deserve to be organized as corporations. An empirical survey follows of the diverse environments in which the public corporation works all the world over; and some explanation is offered of the differences in its status in different countries. Finally there is a discussion of the role of the corporation in an underdeveloped economy.

## 1. *The nature of the public corporation*

The distinctive features of this form of organization may be analysed under four heads: (a) legal, (b) management, (c) economic, and (d) policy.

(a) *Legal.* Firstly, the corporation is the result of a particular statute or Royal Charter, as in the case of the British Broadcasting Corporation. Three factors may account for this, viz., the experimental nature of the method, the relatively small number of enterprises organized as public enterprises and the necessity to pay special

---

[1] For a full account of the development of the public corporation idea in Britain, see G. N. Ostergaard's paper, "Labour and the development of the public corporation", *The Manchester School*, May 1954.

attention to the particular problems of an individual industry. Though the last consideration seems to justify the technique of individual enactments, there is no intrinsic reason against the gradual emergence of some kind of general legislation, analogous to company law, under which all corporations may be registered, and which defines their characteristics, privileges and responsibilities in broad terms, leaving the rules applicable to each particular enterprise to be covered by subordinate documents analogous to a company's memorandum and articles of association. This is likely to happen as the corporations increase in number and greater experience of their problems is gained. Trends in this direction are visible in countries like the U.S.A. and Canada, where attempts have been made to bring the many corporations under a common law in certain matters of government control and public accountability. The recent inclusion in the Indian Companies Act of provisions specifically relating to government companies may be treated as another form of the same trend, though as yet it is the government companies rather than the public corporations to which the legislation refers.[1]

Secondly, the corporation can sue and be sued and has a legal personality distinct from that of the Government. The clearest example of this is shown by section 38 of the Electricity Act, 1957, which provides that "it is hereby declared for the avoidance of doubt that neither the Electricity Council nor the Generating Board nor any of the Area Boards are to be regarded as the servant or agent of the Crown or as enjoying any status, immunity or privileges of the Crown, and no property of the Council or any of these Boards is to be regarded as property of, or held on behalf of, the Crown".[2] The corporation is free from the normal (and generally standardized) rules of working provided for the government departments, with regard to such matters as employment, promotion, pensions and, in many cases, annual budgets and auditing. In other words, it is a public enterprise free from government routine in its working.

(b) *Management*. The corporation represents a special case of the separation of ownership from management, the directors being generally nominated by the Minister.[3] They are not elected at a meeting of the shareholders; and in fact, the general public who constitute the shareholders lose their identity to the point of being represented by the Minister. The removal of the appointing right from the

[1] Sections 617–620 of the Indian Companies Act refer to the government companies registered under the Act.

[2] The position is less clear in the U.S.A., where the Supreme Court's rulings have been different at different times.

[3] The London Passenger Transport Board was an exception. The Boards of all post-war corporations are constituted by the appropriate Ministers.

investors' hands is the vital point,[1] though appointment by the Minister does not follow as invariably necessary.[2] There is no reason to suppose that, with the wider and more common use of the corporation method, the machinery of appointments would remain exactly what it is today. In course of time, the major bulk of the task of selection may be entrusted to some special appointments commission. With greater success in defining the matters to be decided by the Minister on the one hand and the Boards on the other,[3] there would be less need than at present to keep the Board members constantly amenable to Ministerial influence. It would then follow that the Minister need not be the exclusive appointing authority. To set up an appointing machinery placing emphasis on the criterion of efficiency is desirable. It may still be necessary to retain for the Minister powers of final approval in order to ensure the most appropriate combination of skills and of levels of skills to be invited from outside and to give effect to certain value judgements which may be called for by the ruling circumstances of the industry from time to time—e.g., specially bad industrial relations or lack of leadership; yet the major part of his influence could gradually be integrated into the general framework of the appointing machinery, so that this personality exerts itself no further than to the minimum extent necessary in the normal working of the machinery. The establishment of an appointments commission to assist in the formation of Boards would help in relieving the possibility and allegation of the Minister filling the Boards with his own men,[4] perhaps lacking in independence, as in Greece.[5]

[1] In the case of some Indian corporations, however, where representation of interests has been adopted, some directors are nominated or elected by specific investor-groups, e.g., by the Reserve Bank, the scheduled banks, the co-operative banks, etc., in the case of the Industrial Finance Corporation.

[2] In fact the London Passenger Transport Board and the Port of London Authority have not been constituted by the Minister at all.

[3] See section 3 in the present Chapter and Chapter III.

[4] There are a few, though still infrequent, traces of rethinking on the important question of Board appointments in Great Britain. Lord Reith suggested, in his paper "Public corporations: need to examine control and structure", *Public Administration*, Winter 1956, a permanent public appointments commission "to advise the Crown".

Mr. Palmer asked in Parliament, "But how are the leaders of these industries being appointed? What is the system which is followed? That seems to me a legitimate question to put. . . . I do not want to put this too unkindly, but does the 'old pals' club' work on occasions?" (*Hansard*, Vol. 578, col. 1110).

[5] One extreme possibility under the system of Ministerial appointment is illustrated by Greece where "a change of Ministry brings a change of directors, for they are held to occupy political posts, even though they are not expected to engage in active politics". (George D. Daskalki, "Public Enterprise in Greece", in *Public Enterprise*, edited by A. H. Hanson, p. 234.) He mentions as one of the conditions of better management that "politics" must be "eliminated from the processes of appointment and promotion" (p. 237).

Secondly, the corporation is distinguished, in the field of management, by the fact that the Board is under no constant check of shareholders or owners and that it is ultimately responsible to the Minister and Parliament.[1] In its day-to-day working the situation is analogous to that of large private units whose shareholders are not in a position to check the Board's working, though the Board's ultimate responsibility is to them in the long run. (Of course the Board has to reckon with the city press comments which are available.)

The third managerial feature of the corporation is that the Board is answerable for its operations in terms of given factual criteria and is free from the bias of political considerations.[2] This is what is sometimes described as a "self-denying" act of Parliament, in the sense that it has consciously denied itself the right of intervention in the corporations in so far as they are of a commercial character.

(c) *Economic*. It is normally fundamental to the idea of a corporation that a reasonable relationship between cost and price is contemplated and that it is required to operate under conditions of financial self-support, rather than depend on subsidy. The objective rationale of its operations is derived from the understanding that, in the absence of contrary directions from the Government, prices should be based on "related" costs, region by region and consumer group by group. It would be sufficient, at this stage, to assume as given a framework of cost-price relationship.[3]

Secondly, the corporation should have a fair degree of autonomy of financial appropriation. It should be enabled, on its own initiative and decision, to decide on the raising of funds, plan out its annual budget, choose among the available operating alternatives and formulate reserve and reserve appropriation policies, though (i) its aggregate financial ends, including self-financing limits, ought to be set by the Government or statute, and (ii) care should be taken to prevent the Board's operations from having implications of social policy. (In practice, however, the financial arrangements are more restrictive in many countries.)

---

[1] Once again the London Passenger Transport Board was an exception.

[2] For example, most of the corporation Acts in India lay down that "it shall be the general principle of a corporation that in carrying on its undertaking it shall act on business principles" (section 22 of the Road Transport Corporations Act, 1950).

[3] There are two important and controversial questions needing a general answer of guidance for the Boards: marginal cost pricing and discrimination. At this stage of describing the characteristics of a corporation a two-fold assumption is made, viz., that an answer is found and that it is expected to be followed by the Boards.

18

A third characteristic follows. The corporation can choose the best among alternative courses of action open to it in a given situation, on clearly defined factual grounds, unlike the civil servant heading a department of Government and working constantly under Ministerial, i.e., political, influence. This is what facilitates public assessment of its performance.

(d) *Policy*. There are two other essentials of a corporation to which enough systematic attention has not yet been paid. Firstly, a corporation requires a division of the powers needed for the full performance of its functions, among Parliament, the Minister, the Board and its lower levels. The division is far from easy to make. Some of the complex factors to be considered are that Parliament's powers ought to be confined to broad policy enunciation and ultimate control; the Minister, who should form an important means of constructive vigilance and oversight, is a party man with a relatively short-term interest in the results of the corporation and that the conferment of all power and responsibility on a single statutory apex body may work in practice against the right pattern of power devolution inside the corporation, while the statutory diffusion of power and responsibility over the different levels below the central body may create an undesirable friction in the working of the enterprise. Although it is true that a rigid and thorough division is not possible in every case, some answer is provided by a rough classification of industrial performance into three sections: (i) over-all objects and policies involving obviously value judgements; (ii) decisions regarding "means" (i.e., the methods adopted for achieving the objects and broad policies); and (iii) operating matters. The first category constitutes the prerogative of Parliament; while the third is clearly internal to the Board.

If Parliament is content with the first category, the corporation would in practice tend to function in the manner of a private enterprise working under the ordinary provisions of government control. If, on the other hand, Parliament limits the Board to the last category of power, the corporation works in practice as a replica of a department, except for certain obvious, though minor, differences as in the form of accounts or audit. Neither is ideal, however; and the real value of a corporation rests on where the intermediate category regarding means is located, with a view to preventing an unintended assumption by the Board of parliamentary prerogatives as well as an undesirable intervention by Parliament in the Board's working. Herein lies the kernel of autonomy.

It is true that the difficulties of locating this category of power would be fewer than at present, if we formulate clear rules which would hold the Boards from decisions with policy consequences[1]—point for later discussion; and the sources of public discontent could correspondingly be narrowed down. There is, however, a more fundamental difficulty. The factual and apparently objective decisions of the Board have an eventual influence on the formulation of over-all objects and policies; for, decision-making being a continuous process, at any given time over-all objects cannot be fixed or altered by Parliament, without being conditioned by (the consequences of) means-decisions (decisions in the process of achieving the objects) already taken by the Board. To take an example, is the issue of closing a colliery to be rated as a factual, internal decision for the Board[2] or as one involving value judgements touching on employment policy? The Board would tend towards a decision of that kind through other incidental means decisions like arrangements for output expansion elsewhere, withdrawal of mobile outlays from the pit marked down for closing and inflow of outside supplies to the local markets. If Parliament takes notice only at the time of closure, it would be too late to reverse the decision made by the Board in good faith after careful consideration, except at the cost of upsetting a series of the Board's methods of working. No rules could ever be sufficiently clear or elaborate in dividing responsibility in this field between the Minister and the Board; and it is possible that certain issues worthy of parliamentary attention resolve themselves into Board decisions in practice while others which deserve to be Board decisions may have parliamentary attention focused on them. The distinction between policy and day-to-day administration has been a useful platitude in the experimental stages of the corporation method.[3] The time has

---

[1] For example, Gilbert Walker and H. Maddick point out the diffusion of responsibility for transport and urge "that the responsibilities for deciding policies, which affect the nation economically, strategically and socially, should no longer be laid on the Commission but should be shouldered and discharged by the Minister subject to parliamentary control". ("Responsibility for Transport", *Political Quarterly*, July–September 1952, p. 234.)

Certain decisions taken by the Boards on their assumption that broader interests are required to be watched by them, are strictly of a question-begging character; for they cannot assume, unless told by the Minister, that they in particular were expected to take the particular decisions they took, and they are liable to be criticized if such decisions resulted in deficits or other results that violated the spirit or letter of the Acts.

[2] In answer to a question in Parliament, Gaitskell, Minister of Fuel and Power, said: "I think we can leave these matters to the National Coal Board and the National Union of Mine Workers to settle." (*Hansard*, Vol. 454, cols. 556–7.)

[3] Marshall E. Dimock observes: "there is an important area of sub-policy and decision-making midway between the over-all action of Congress and the point where the administrator takes up. It is this area that a representative and resourceful board of directors must occupy if government corporations are to operate with efficiency and accountability." ("Government corporations: a focus of policy

come when it should be examined from the practical point of view.

At this stage it is necessary to note, though briefly, the meaning of "decisions with policy implications". Three broad categories may be distinguished. (a) In the field of pricing, clear meaning is possible, in the sense of decisions deviating from cost considerations or introducing discriminations not based on cost considerations. Evidently this is a complicated definition, on which more will be said in Chapter III. (b) In the field of factor combination and internal composition of the industry (in terms of plant sizes, numbers and location)—e.g., the use of British coal or liquid gas for gasification,[1] the closure of a coal mine and mechanization affecting labour, the reference is to those decisions that are not objectively derived on grounds of cost economy. It may be that the data for adjudging these decisions are not always to hand but involve guesses on untried alternatives. (c) Then there are the more complicated decisions which touch on broad social questions—e.g., appropriation of surpluses for workers' welfare, standards of comfort (in housing, etc.) provided for the workers, the other employees and the top men.[2] Objective norms are impossible in this field; and value judgements are bound to exist in establishing whether a decision of the Board has consequences which Parliament does not relish.

Secondly, the corporation method calls for a division of responsibility for results between the Minister and the Board. Little progress has been made in public discussion—and less in legislative action—in this respect. If it is accepted that the Board is not the final arbiter of corporation performance, the Board cannot be held solely responsible for the results of working; and the success of the corporation method[3] depends on the segregation of results traceable to the Board's own decisions from the results of external decisions—e.g., Ministerial directions or certain statutory requirements. It is implicit in the basic motive of "freedom from political interference" that the

---

and administration", *American Political Science Review*, October 1949.) Unfortunately, it is exactly in this area that the difficulties described above arise.

[1] Alfred Robens commented on the liquefied gas experiment of the Gas Council, referred to its effect on the British coal industry, and asked, "have they looked at all the things involved?" (*Hansard*, H.C. Vol. 578, col. 1026.)

[2] Some samples are: the allocation of £10,000 assigned to the members of the National Coal Board for their expenses and the transport provided for them in London, the purchase of Himley Hall by the Midland Divisional Coal Board, the advertising techniques adopted by the Boards and the purchase of "large and luxurious" houses for senior officials. On all these questions the Minister, Mr. Shinwell, denied responsibility in Parliament in 1946. But there are many who have at least ideological concern with these questions.

[3] The term "success of the corporation method" ought not to be confused with the success of a corporation in the sense of high profits.

corporation by itself is not to take such decisions as are generally taken under the influence of politics. It should, therefore, follow as a corollary that conditions must be created for verifying if the corporation has fulfilled this expectation.

The public corporation is an institution without a homogeneous legal form (unlike a joint stock company, for example); no wonder it has been variously conceived.[1] The common feature of most descriptions is that it combines private status and ability with public purpose and responsibility. The latter is not wholly absent in the case of private enterprise;[2] but it is dependent on the interpretation of public purpose by private businessmen, governmental persuasion and, in the end, government regulation, *ad hoc* or otherwise.[3] On the other hand, the public corporation can be looked upon as a far more convenient vehicle of public policies—or else, there is no reason to displace private enterprise. Yet it is not necessarily to constitute a constant and automatic medium of government policies; for this purpose de-

---

[1] One of the earliest definitions was by President Roosevelt. He termed the Tennessee Valley Authority as a "corporation clothed with the power of government but possessed of the flexibility and initiative of a private enterprise". (In his Message to Congress in 1933.)

President Truman: "Experience indicates that the corporate form of organization is peculiarly adapted to the administration of governmental programmes which are predominantly of a commercial character—those which are revenue producing, are at least potentially self-sustaining, and involve a large number of business-type transactions with the public." (Budget Message for 1948.)

The Brownlow Commission: "Its particular value lies in freedom of operation, flexibility, business efficiency, and opportunity for experimentation . . . Particularly in the case of permanent, as opposed to emergency, corporations, freedom of operation finds justification in the fact that they are financially self-sustaining. The balance sheet incentive is present to insure efficient and economical administration without the imposition of the usual Government controls." (President's Committee on Administrative Management, Report with Special Studies, p. 302.)

R. Darcy Best, with reference to the U.K. Atomic Energy Authority, observed: It combines "the freedom and flexibility of an industrial enterprise with operation under strict government control". (*Public Administration*, Spring 1956, p. 1.)

[2] Referring to the reconciliation of commercial and non-commercial considerations in the conduct of industrial management, Herbert Morrison observed: "under modern conditions private industry is doing this every day. (a) Its commercial freedom is limited by Government controls. (b) British industry is by no means unresponsive to governmental persuasion where the public interest is involved. (c) And it is often bad commercial practice—bad labour relations and bad public relations—to pursue the profit motive without regard to broader social considerations." (*Public Administration*, Spring 1950, p. 4.)

[3] For example, to serve the public interest of locating economic activity in the distressed areas, the Government set up a general framework of regulation under the Distribution of Industry Act of 1945. Specific instances of purposive governmental regulation are building licences.

partmental organization is preferable. It is in preserving its autonomy subject to the guarantee of contemplated public purposes that its merit as a method remains; otherwise it ends up as the proverbial Cheshire cat.[1] And the concept of autonomy should be broader than "the privilege", in Dimock's words, "of being left alone so long as you do not overstep the rules laid down in advance",[2] and have reference to the "area" within the rules laid down. This logically leads us to the next stage of our discussion: what is the purpose of government control over the corporation?

## 2. *The choice of the corporation method*

Let us examine, as a preliminary to the discussion on control, the considerations that ought to determine the choice of the corporation form as against departmental organization.

Firstly, is flexibility in the managerial structure a desired value? If it is, the corporation seems to be preferable for two reasons. (a) It permits of a variety of principles being followed in the constitution of the Board, including that of representation of interests, as in France and in some cases in India. This would be nearly impossible with the departmental organization, except for the medium of an advisory body, as in the case of the British Post Office. (b) The managerial Board can be composed of full-time and part-time men, functional and policy men, and of such special skills as may be particularly deemed desirable from time to time. If such flexibility is a virtue, as it is with private enterprise, it could be retained within limits in the case of a corporation.

An incidental advantage is that the corporation provides greater opportunities for the formation of managerial skill at the intermediate and growing levels, it being assumed that the personnel policies are not identically the same as those of the department and that the managerial cadre is permitted to function with sufficient autonomy; and this is one of its greatest long-term merits. The Indian situation, as described by P. H. Appleby, illustrates the unfavourable environment in which the departmental managers tend to act. "The Members of Parliament greatly exaggerate the importance of the function of the Comptroller and Auditor-General, and pay far too much attention to his reports. So doing, Parliament increases the

---

[1] Referring to the American government corporations, Herman Pritchett thought as early as in 1941 that the distinguishing features of the corporation were "disappearing before our eyes, like the Cheshire cat. Soon there may be nothing left but a smile to mark the spot where the government corporation once stood." ("The paradox of the government corporation," *Public Administration Review*, Summer 1941, p. 389.)

[2] Marshall E. Dimock, *American Political Science Review*, October 1949, p. 913.

timidity of public servants at all levels, making them unwilling to take responsibility for decisions, forcing decisions to be made by a slow and cumbersome process of reference and conference in which everybody finally shares dimly in the making of every decision, not enough gets done and what gets done is done too slowly." There is in fact a negative, but strong, administrative ground against departmental organization of commercial enterprises in a country like India. Parliament is a new institution and the right kind of traditions as to delegation of powers are yet to be formed. At the moment "Parliament is a chief citadel of opposition to delegation of powers, the need for which is the worst shortcoming of Indian administration. Parliament's reluctance to delegate its powers in detail, as it is essential to do if Parliamentary powers are to be important and positive, discourages Ministers from delegating their powers, discourages Secretaries from delegating their powers, and Managing Directors from delegating their powers."[1] As long as the desirable degree of delegation is wanting—and it would take a long time firmly to establish its roots, in any case—the corporation method would be one method of relieving the enterprise from an administratively defective framework.

Secondly, is an elaborate central planning of the industry contemplated? This is different from general economic planning and refers to the deliberate decisions taken at the apex in substitution for, or serious subordination of, the price mechanism and the consumer's freedom of choice. Departmental organization implies an emphasis on uniform practice, non-competitive operations, and the avoidance of any apparent symptom of lack of co-ordination. The corporation enjoys far greater latitude in its operations, though it works within the broad criteria of targets set by the Government or Parliament.

Thirdly, is the public enterprise expected to work mainly on commercial principles, as opposed to the canons of taxation and of social policy? If it is, the corporation form is desirable. It is true that neither the corporation is totally free from the canons of taxation and of social policy, nor is the departmental organization totally free from commercial principles. Yet the relative emphasis is different in the two cases. For example, a patient who takes more of the doctor's time than another for the same complaint is not charged more just for that reason; though a consumer of ten units of electricity is charged more than one consuming five, other things being equal—like the time of consumption.

The commercial basis of the enterprise applies to pricing, decisions on capital outlays and dealings with labour, purchase of inputs and

[1] P. H. Appleby, *Re-examination of India's administrative system with special reference to administration of Government's industrial and commercial enterprises.* 1956, pp. 44–5.

so on. Many nationalization measures are not specifically taken with the desire of imposing gross value judgements or political decisions in these matters; and certain values like labour welfare and managerial opportunities for the working class are indeed independent of the nature of enterprise and its form. Where the motive is limited to the prevention of private capital gains or the removal of private monopoly power, or where the reason for nationalization is the need to improve the industry's efficiency or, more specifically, to improve the industrial relations or increase investment, it is desirable to form a corporation and leave it free to manage the industry in the ordinary commercial way, once provision is made for the specifically desired remedy.

Fourthly, what is the extent of political control desired and how continuous is it intended to be? If there is no general agreement in favour of rigid and continuous control, the corporation is the preferable form. Of course the answer to this, as also to the second and third questions above, depends on whether the industry is considered as of such a basic character as calls for a heavy admixture of commercial and social values in most of its operations and decisions; and whether this cannot be achieved by appropriate rules or ministerial directions to the corporation. These points should be positively proved, and not merely assumed. The corporation method, incidentally, helps in revealing to the public the costs of social policy wherever it is sought to be imposed, if clear information is available on the policy imposed and its consequences; and the Government would impose a policy only after serious deliberation.

Experience shows that unanimity of view does not generally prevail on the last three questions, even amongst members of a political party in favour of nationalization; still less is there consensus of opinion between members of different parties. There is another anomaly, viz., that a party which is opposed to nationalization in general has, on coming to power, to decide on the nationalized industries' policies. As long as there is strong opposition to the cult of automatism in the central planning of an industry, the substitution of social policy for commercial principles, and elaborate and continuous political control, the corporation method has the utility of preventing the public enterprise from becoming a political weapon in the hands of the party in power, though it cannot prevent any specific governmental intervention.

Two general arguments may be added in support of the corporation method. The more the public enterprises and the greater the proportion of the economy brought into the public sector, the wider is the area liable to centralized decision, co-ordination and planning. Such centralized administration tends to be ill-done for obvious human reasons (the wood being missed for the trees), unless they take the shape of broad policy determination and occasional *ad hoc* intervention. Both of these are possible with the corporation method; and the corporation retains at least a great part of the self-adjusting processes characteristic, though imperfectly today, of private industrial organization. Though public enterprise intends to "order" the benefits of the industrial activity, it need not necessarily write off all its ordinary internal processes; such an attempt might often affect the quantum of benefits themselves.

Lastly, the corporation method has an invaluable political merit in a democracy where economic totalitarianism is far from being accepted as valuable. Even if the public sector is large or continually expanding, the corporation method minimizes the undue concentration of power in the hands of the cabinet or the ruling party.

### 3. *The rationale of government control*

The questions raised in this section are: What are the purposes that the Government intends the corporation to achieve? How directly are the means of ensuring the desired objects linked with government control? What forms may government control take? Finally, what are the consequential arrangements necessary if the corporation is to work distinctively as a corporation?

1. The primary concern of the Government is to ensure that the objects with which the corporation is set up are fulfilled. In a simple sense it is for the Government, representing the collective ownership of the industry, to exercise its right of making the Board, which has no special or direct ownership interest, adhere to the basic objectives and policies of the owner. (Even under private enterprise, company laws have been amended from time to time, e.g., in India, with the purpose of preventing undue passage of power, with potentialities of abuse, from the owners to the managers, or "managing agents" in the Indian context.) While there can be no controversy about this motive, it is not clear that it should lead to elaborate government control. If the powers over appointment and dismissal of Board members are retained in the Government's hands, the right course of action would be to create the conditions conducive to the best results. (The nature of the machinery needed for this purpose will be discussed in the chapter on public accountability.)

This is analogous to W. A. Robson's description that "the essential functions of a Government department dealing with a nationalized industry are to measure its performance, to see that it keeps technically up to date and economically efficient, and to ensure that it is operated in such a manner as to provide the greatest amount of service to the largest possible number of consumers at the minimum cost consistent with financial self-support".[1]

The suggestion that no direct government control is necessary for this purpose presupposes two conditions. Firstly, the functions with which the Board is charged ought not to be a mixture of commercial and social purposes as illustrated by phrases[2] like "an efficient, adequate, economical and properly integrated system of public inland transport"[3] or "as may seem to them (the National Coal Board) best calculated to further the public interest".[4] If the objectives include closely integrated commercial and social purposes, it is at least controversial as to whether Parliament should delegate to any outside machinery, however competent, the power of ensuring the intended results; and the way would be clear for constant exercise of government control.[5] The second condition is that the intended results of the public enterprise should be expressed in sufficient clarity in the provisions of the Act, or, in the interests of flexibility, in ministerial regulations. This may not be an easy task; for apart from the difficulties of accurate draftsmanship, it is likely that, while nationalization is effected for vaguely understood ideological purposes, there is not sufficient unanimity about the purposes for these to be written into the Act. (Even within the nationalizing party, vital differences may prevail in this respect; and in the interests of the eventual success of the enactment the viewpoint of the other parties cannot be totally ignored.)

These two conditions must be satisfied in order that the corporation method may succeed, the more so as pragmatic arguments replace ideological grounds for nationalization.[6]

2. A stronger argument in favour of government control arises

---

[1] W. A. Robson, "The administration of nationalized industries in Britain", *Public Administration Review*, Summer 1947, p. 166.

[2] Such phrases, it is true, may satisfy Parliament, as they openly give expression to the notion of the public interest; and even if they are, therefore, included in the Acts, they could be made to serve as ideological preambles if clearer purposes and rules of behaviour are set for the Boards in the course of the Acts.

[3] Section 3 (1), Transport Act, 1947. Commenting on the unremunerative services within the area of the London Transport Executive, the Chambers Committee observe that the Executive "take the view that under the Acts they are the arbiters of the public need for transport". (Report of the Committee of Inquiry into London Transport, 1955, p. 17.)

[4] Section 1 (1) (b), Coal Nationalization Act, 1947.

[5] The position of the National Coal Board in this respect has been indicated by the Chairman in his evidence to the Select Committee on Nationalized Industries. He observed: "What are we? We are not flesh, fish or good red herring. We are not a commercial undertaking; we are not a public service; we are a bit of each." (Q. 911, Report, 1958.)

[6] There is sufficient evidence of this in Hugh Gaitskell's Fabian Tract, *Socialism and Nationalization* (1956).

from the fact that, in spite of careful legislation, some of the Board decisions have the implication of value judgements—a point made earlier in connection with the intermediate area of means-decisions. Parliament ought rightly to be concerned with arresting the unintended social repercussions of certain Board decisions; and, in the words of Herbert Morrison, Board "Chairmen must not become arbitrary Emperors of Industry".[1] This may be termed the negative ground for intervention, which is a defensible one. (In fact the Labour Party is building up the power argument even in relation to private enterprise, where it is alleged that the "capitalists" exercise power "irresponsibly"[2] and that, in view of the "virtual absence of shareholder control", the boards of directors "exercise enormous power without being responsible to anybody"; and they propose a revision of the Companies' Acts so as to "develop more definite forms of public accountability".[3]

The Government's relationship may be shown in two ways. Firstly, rules may be written into the Act or regulations framed by the Minister from time to time, which classify for the Board's guidance situations potential of social consequences, and the approved priorities or preferences between alternative courses of action may be laid down. Obviously these cannot cover every situation; but they go a long way in narrowing down the area of differences in the intentions of Parliament and the decisions of the Board. For example, the criteria to be faced before a coal-mine is closed—e.g., the extent of unemployment caused and of the alternative arrangements for the absorption of the initially displaced persons—or before a branch line is abandoned—e.g., the possibilities of operating alternative road services by the B.T.C., if necessary—may be specified in broad terms. More concrete rules are suggested in the case of electricity pricing in Chapter III.

The other method is for the Minister to issue directions as and when he discovers the necessity to prevent a certain social consequence. It is, on the whole, wise to limit this method to exceptional circumstances and depend, instead, on a general framework of rules of guidance. For one thing, it is not easy to prove that an avoidable social consequence was imminent; and for another, an *ad hoc* decision may come too sharply against and at the end of a series of allied sub-decisions by the Board upsetting its plans of work.

Ministerial directions may be more commonly issued in those cases where the Government positively wishes to affect a Board decision with social bias. As far as broad categories of operations involving

---

[1] Herbert Morrison, *Government and Parliament*, p. 265.
[2] Hugh Gaitskell, *Socialism and Nationalization*, p. 10.
[3] The Labour Party's pamphlet, *Industry and Society*, p. 49.

particular lines of social policy could be foreseen—e.g., rural electrification—it would be better to prepare general rules of guidance, so that the Board may proceed on those lines as if in its own routine, without receiving a series of *ad hoc* decisions. In all other situations where individual decisions need qualification, there ought to be no alternative to ministerial direction. Incidentally the direction ensures full knowledge for Parliament of the value judgements made by the Minister and fortifies ministerial responsibility to Parliament.

3. A corporation entrusted with the management of a whole industry virtually plans out, by means of conscious decisions, all operations at any given unit of time as well as the growth of the industry over time. It is unlikely that, apart from inevitable mistakes which may be expected in planning on such a large scale, value judgements are made at several points, the more so when the Board does not operate under the influence of an effective price mechanism. Under these circumstances it is necessary to limit the autonomy of the Board. But it does not follow that the Government should assume the Board's functions in this regard, for the Government's deliberate decisions may be no better than the Board's, except that the value judgements are made on the full responsibility of Parliament. It is in this field of unified operations and development planning that an intrinsically sound mechanism analogous, if not equal, to the impersonal co-ordination of the market has yet to be evolved. One thing is certain, viz., that the arrangement whereby the Board has to settle its capital expenditure programmes in consultation with, or subject to, the Minister, is neither the whole nor final answer. It may be necessary to promote other important conditions; e.g., (a) adequate competition within the working of the nationalized industry—where it is wasteful or physically impossible, regional comparisons, subject to the necessary qualifications, must be of value as a guide to investment decisions; (b) improved facilities for consumers as a whole to challenge the price level and the price structures of the industry; and (c) autonomy in the Board's commercial operations. If these are fostered, the Government can limit itself to certain major aspects and ensure that the corporation works with a public purpose, yet without the disadvantage of too much public decision.

4. It is often contended that a corporation which depends on subsidy renders itself automatically liable to government control, since it involves a demand on the general exchequer,[1] which Parlia-

[1] In his evidence before the Select Committee on Nationalized Industries in 1953, Sir Frank N. Tribe, Comptroller and Auditor-General, referred to the possibility of a corporation making a deficit and invoking the Treasury guarantee and said, "Parliament would then have been committed to this expenditure out of the Consolidated Fund without really having known where it was going." (Q. 92, The Report.)

ment would not be willing to meet for purposes not under its own control. In dealing with this argument we have to be clear as to whether the corporation in question is expected to be self-supporting or to carry out a governmental policy not worked on full-cost pricing principle—e.g., housing subsidies. In the latter case the corporation form is of nominal value, except to ensure freedom in the technical aspects of carrying out given jobs. This limited freedom can be assured even inside a department, as it is in the Public Works Departments. In the case of the corporations which are expected to be (at least) self-sufficient, Parliament's chief interest must be to ensure that they are so. Control in the event of deficits should be a secondary consideration.[1]

The question of deficits needs further examination. These may result from (a) the nature of the industry, e.g., aviation; (b) over-capitalization, e.g., due to heavy compensation and structural changes; (c) short run or cyclical factors; (d) inefficient management; and (e) social policy, e.g., unremunerative but essential transport services. The first condition requires subsidies, but need not call for government control for that reason only provided that it is believed by Parliament that, with the best of management, a deficit is inevitable and that nevertheless the industry must continue to exist on the scale proposed. It would in fact be desirable to fix the subsidy and expect the Board to attain results which, supplemented by the subsidy, would meet all revenue charges including interest. In the second case, Parliament may write off the capital figure appropriately[2] and require the corporation not to make a deficit under the new conditions, rather than use the inability of the corporation to meet the interest charges on the over-capitalization as an argument for exercising control. If Parliament is not inclined to write off the loss, the straightforward course would be to let the corporation exercise its monopoly power, if any, to earn enough to cover the costs of over-capitalization, rather than to prevent it from doing so and make the consequent deficits an excuse for more control. If the deficits are due to temporary or cyclical conditions, the best course would be to let the corporation work out its own reserve and financial policies, so that Parliament is relieved of the subsidy-burden either in any year or "taking one year with another". Where inefficient management

---

[1] The concern of the Treasury in the case of deficits may be illustrated by reference to A. T. K. Grant's evidence before the Select Committee on Nationalized Industries, 1957. He said, "As long as the Nationalized Industry is doing all right we are much less concerned, but we would feel that if losses are being made we would want to know about the price policy and we would want to take a great deal more interest . . . in the question of losses as compared with the general one of price rises." (Q. 150.)

[2] See Chapter VI.

leads to losses, the only solution lies in overhauling the Board and its lower levels, perhaps calling for the advice of management experts; and there is little that extra control by Parliament could achieve in that situation. In the last case of social policy leading to deficits, the best answer is to assess the consequences of the external influence on the Board's operations and recompute the financial results of the corporation after providing for them. Where the intrusion of social policy is too elaborate to permit a proper assessment of its consequences, it is perhaps an equally good step to run the enterprise as a government department rather than raise, without solving, delicate problems of the half-way house of the corporation.

It may now be seen that the argument of government control in a situation of subsidies calls for certain basic decisions on Parliament's part regarding the financial status of the corporation.[1] Control may be an easy tool to grab but basically the problem needs a solution beyond the wielding of control by the Government.

5. The most difficult argument for government control arises on grounds of general economic and social policy. In its simplest version, it emphasizes the need for consistency between government policy and the operations of the corporations. One may term this an essentially American argument. In the words of the Hoover Commission, "the significant differences between business enterprises and other government activities do not relate to *purpose*, but are to be found in the *nature* of the activity, operating practices, methods of *financing*, and internal organization."[2] The importance of consistency is implicit in Leonard White's observation that "the policy of the government as a whole shall be free from contradiction".[3] The argument must have

---

[1] How vague Parliament's attitude to the financial status of the corporations could be is illustrated by Noel-Baker's observation on the French railways: "In France I believe the deficit which is paid by Parliament every year is about £120 million in our currency, but that I believe is not at all a matter of policy because it is in the interests of the nation but it is just because no Minister has ever had the courage to come along and say the fares ought to be raised." (Report from the Select Committee on Nationalized Industries, 1953, Q. 136.)

[2] The Hoover Report, *Federal Business Enterprises*, pp. 94–5, 1945.

[3] L. White, *Introduction to the Study of Public Administration*, p. 122. Further evidence of the view is plentifully available from American writings. H. Seidman observes that private and government corporations "both have a legal personality, can sue and be sued, and generally have boards of directors. Here the resemblance ends. Private corporations, with the obvious exceptions, are organized for profit. . . . Government corporations are organized to achieve a public purpose authorized by law. This fact is often forgotten. So far as purpose is concerned, a corporation cannot be distinguished from any other government agency. . . . The functions of a corporation are the same as those of any administrative agency; the difference between the two is in the *method* employed to perform the functions." (*Public Administration Review*, Autumn 1953, p. 93.)

S. D. Goldberg and H. Seidman observe, "a government corporation, unlike

31

derived from the fact that many of the government corporations in the U.S.A. were the creatures of emergency, war and depression, meant to carry out a governmental purpose in an expeditious manner. In Great Britain, however, the trend of thought has on the whole been different; and nationalization has in large measure been justified on "efficiency" grounds relating to the individual industries.[1]

On deeper examination, the "consistency" argument turns out to be a complicated one; for, with a change in government it may call for a change in the corporation's working policies—just the antithesis of good commercial practice which the corporation form is expected to foster. The corporation must be free from this possibility, though the Government should be free to set its major objectives and give specific directions where necessary. This is not a plea for insulating the corporations totally from the Government's economic policies; however, they should be touched neither more than the industrial system in general nor more than on their own merits, irrespective of public ownership.

Secondly, a case is made out for government intervention in order that there may be co-ordination among the nationalized industries. The fuel industries are a good illustration. If carefully analysed, the contention has three aspects. (i) The case for co-ordination must rest, if at all, on the nature of the industries concerned and the situation in which they are found to be working at the given time. The fact that they are nationalized does not constitute a specific ground for co-ordination. (ii) To ask for co-ordination because it is possible under common government ownership of the industries concerned, is to ask for a monopoly practice. And motives apart, all the weaknesses and dangers of monopoly as an economic institution present them-

---

a private corporation, is merely one cog in a very complex machine. If the machine is to operate smoothly and not break down, some one must see that all the cogs are properly meshed together." (*The Government Corporation: Elements of a Model Charter*, 1953.)

M. E. Dimock asks: "How can the government plan its economic programmes unless such operations are subject to the same executive control, thus obviating the danger of contradictory or unco-operative courses of actions?" (*The American Political Science Review*, December 1949, p. 1149.)

The Supreme Court observed in the Cherry Cotton Mills case that the corporation is chosen "to accomplish purely governmental purposes".

[1] Hugh Gaitskell observes, "indeed it is a most striking fact that in presenting the case for nationalizing the industries transferred to public ownership between 1945 and 1950, the Labour Party spokesmen relied far less on the traditional arguments and far more on practical considerations designed to show that nationalization was the best or only way to achieve higher production, greater efficiency and protection against monopoly." (*Socialism and Nationalization*, p. 18.)

selves under the garb of co-ordination.[1] (iii) A temporary measure deemed necessary in the interests of one of the industries or all of them or in the national interest can always be implemented by specific government action through directions; and no continuing control would be necessary for this purpose.

The British experiments with nationalization have generally been free from the employment of government control as a means of inter-industry co-ordination.[2] Certain possibilities of inter-industry sub-sidization, which are not illegal, have not been exploited, e.g., low electricity rates to railways.[3] The denationalization of road haulage has weakened the original enthusiasm for monolithic co-ordination in the field of inland transport. With reference to the co-ordinated working of the fuel industries,, the Minister announced in 1957 that "the basis of co-ordination must be competition" and visualized nevertheless "a good deal of Government guidance" which he limited to two purposes—"the balance of payments problem" and "the settling of the capital programmes".[4] The desirability of some fusion of activities at the "consumer end", e.g., in respect of meter-reading and billing,[5] does not constitute a special ground for govern-ment control; it is to be expected that the corporations concerned would, in the interest of economy, explore all possible channels of inter-unit co-operation, just as units in private enterprise do. (In fact there is no reason why either the gas or the electricity industry should not develop economical relationships with any other industry as well, private or public.)

[1] The Paymaster-General, Reginald Maudling, said: "It is not easy to decide from Whitehall at what point competition becomes wasteful and ceases to be what it ought to be, a spur to efficiency of these industries." (*Hansard*, H.C. Vol. 578, col. 1021.)

[2] The Minister for Fuel and Power described it as "a complete misconception of the plan of nationalizing these industries" to think "that all competition between gas and electricity should disappear". (*Hansard*, Vol. 447, p. 227.) "To sum up, co-ordination is not dictation. It is certainly not dictation to the con-sumer and it is not dictation to the Board" (p. 237–8).

[3] For example, the North Western Electricity Consultative Council "were of the opinion that the general conditions of supply" of electricity to the railways "were those normally associated with large industrial supplies and there was no preferential treatment". (Report, 1956–57, para. 13.)

[4] *Hansard*, H.C. Vol. 578, cols. 1019–20.
Also see *Hansard* 529, col. 2512. During the second reading debate on Gas and Electricity (Borrowing Powers) Bill, the Minister said, "The Government's policy is to combine full-blooded competition between the fuel and power industries with co-ordination in the national interest."

[5] For example, Gerald Nabarro suggested "the method of fusing the selling arrangements of the two industries" (gas and electricity) and referred to the possibility of "substantial economies" through "administrative fusion between gas and electricity in their accounting and metering systems and readings, and in their showroom premises". (*Hansard*, Vol. 578, col. 1949.)

A variation of the above argument is that, as the corporations increase in number, government control is necessary in order to avoid glaring asymmetries in their policies and operations.[1] But this falls to the ground if we accept that an industry does not, in its day-to-day operations within the statutory rules, call for specific government direction simply because it is nationalized. The different corporations ought to be free to follow the methods best suited to them. If Parliament expresses preference for any particular method being followed by all the corporations, e.g., Electricity or Gas Boards, it could be written into the Act or expressed in ministerial regulations.

It is contended, with special reference to South and Central America, that too many corporations imply organized power concentrations outside the government departments, reducing the ministries to "hollow shells". H. Seidman observes that "in some parts of Latin America public corporations can be said literally to constitute a headless and irresponsible fourth branch of government".[2] The real implication here is that the countries have too much of public enterprise in their given situations—the need for public enterprise in these under-developed countries may be great, but their ability to cope with its problems is poor; and that what is lacking is a defined purpose of each public enterprise *vis-à-vis* the taxpayer and the consumer whenever an industry is transferred to, or sponsored under, public aegis.[3] The need in these countries is that the broad indications in favour of public enterprise must, at the stage of execution, be replaced by definitive purposes in each individual case. Given these purposes, the statute can be suitably drafted and the corporations let to work as autonomous institutions without the danger of irresponsibility on their part.

The final argument for government control is that the public enterprises could be made the instruments of general economic policy or of economic planning. It is particularly desirable in the case of the

---

[1] An instance of dissimilar practices was given by Tudor Watkins during the debate in the House of Commons on the Gas and Electricity Reports on 26th November, 1957. In the area of Mid-Wales, "we find three boards, each with a separate policy for connection charges. The Merseyside and North Wales Board bases its charges on acreage. The Midlands Board has not a charge, but a guarantee, making up half the difference of guaranteed sum. This is a good arrangement. The South Wales Board, in whose area are many farms to be electrified, has a system of capital contributions. . . . I am sure that it would be a good thing to have uniformity of policy in connection charges." (*Hansard*, Vol. 578, col. 1096.)

[2] H. Seidman, *Public Administration Review*, Spring 1952, p. 96.

[3] As observed by A. H. Hanson, "the problem of achieving the most effective form of co-ordination between planning and execution is one that no Central or South American State has as yet seriously tackled." (*Public Enterprise*, p. 142.)

basic industries that their operations must be conducive to the broader economic interests of the nation. The points at which the public enterprises could be the media of national economic policies are as follows: (i) the level of prices, or, in other words, the surpluses they may aim at; (ii) the structure of prices, i.e., the discriminations in the regional and consumer-group sense; (iii) the employment programmes; (iv) the investment plans; and (v) the appropriation of surplus among re-investment, consumers and workers. It is not impossible to achieve the Government's ends when the enterprises remain private. But the process would not be automatic; and as Herbert Morrison observed, "one of the reasons for socializing the basic industries is that it would not be safe to rely on persuasion to ensure that they conform to national policy; and it has always been understood that there might be circumstances in which they would be required to do things which would not be expected of even the most public-spirited private firm."[1] There is no doubt that the Government would be in a better position with regard to its employment policies by influencing the investment programmes of the public enterprises.[2] Nor is it contested that national policies must be reflected in the entire cross-section of industrial operations in the country, not to speak of the public enterprises only. One could trace the extensive scope for ministerial intervention in the case of the post-war corporations to the planning ideology of the Labour Party.[3] And some feel that "if over-all planning in the Keynesian sense is to have any meaning then autonomy in this context must also take on a new meaning, and not merely be synonymous with ordinary commercial methods of running a business".[4]

Let us now turn to the complications in this field. The primary

[1] "Public control of socialized industries", *Public Administration*, Spring 1950, p. 5.

[2] Hugh Gaitskell: "The government does have much more prospect of speeding up investment in the public than in the private sector." (*Socialism and Nationalization*, p. 33.)

It is contended in the Labour Party's pamphlet entitled *Fifty Facts on Public Ownership* that, "with the basic industries in public hands, the nation now has the power to hold off slumps by stepping up investment in public enterprises if private owners slow their investment down" (p. 5).

[3] H. A. Clegg observed, "The emphasis on the responsibility of Boards through the Minister to Parliament was one of Labour's contributions to the public corporations. It marked a change to an age of economic planning from a period in which the independence of public boards was stressed so heavily that the very power of appointment was taken out of the hands of the Minister in the revised London Passenger Transport Act of 1933," *Public Administration*, Autumn 1955, p. 271.

[4] Margaret Finnegan, "Ministerial Control of Electricité de France", *Public Administration*, Winter 1954, p. 449.

problem in an economy where planning has to compromise heavily with consumers' freedom and producers' competition, is to be clear about the nature and extent of external decisions to be imposed on the corporations. Two questions arise. Firstly, should the decisions springing from national policy apply to the public enterprises only? If so, they may lead to an over-expansion or under-expansion of the industries that happen to be within the public sector; or the brunt of intended results may be borne disproportionately by the public enterprises. In other words, insufficient consideration is given to the desirability or otherwise of employing them as the only or major means. Secondly, what exactly is connoted by the term "public interest"? For example, Alfred Robens argued in Parliament that "the (Gas) Council's main task is to make gas from British coal".[1] This could, with some argument, be linked with the national interest and the balance of payments question. What proves difficult, however, is to draw a line between the issues that comprise the public interest and those that do not, once we proceed to details, beyond such broad principles as full employment or regulated investment programmes.

The next and closely allied problem is how to translate the national interest into the working of the corporation, without destroying its autonomy as regards the means-decisions. It is important to give statutory form, as far as possible, to this idea, so that not only the Board knows its limits of decision-making but the Minister himself cannot easily trespass his own limits *vis-à-vis* Parliament while committing the Board to his decisions or directions. Broadly accepted national policies, i.e., those accepted by Parliament, could be written into the Act or appropriate statutory instruments—e.g., surplus targets or limits, pricing rules reflecting social policies to which effect should or should not be given, investment programmes and major employment policies. As regards the others which may become important from time to time, the Minister should give the necessary directions.

It is at this point that we may touch on one of the basic issues in the field of government control. The Minister's social or economic policy is in the nature of a short run interest for the industry, since the party in power is keen on what happens during its five-year period and has an eye on the following election prospects.[2] On the other

---

[1] *Hansard*, H.C. Vol. 578, col. 1027.

[2] Referring to the Minister's reaction to applications by the National Coal Board for an increase in coal prices, the Select Committee on Nationalized Industries observed, "On the whole the Minister's is a more short-term view than the Board's, and he is affected by considerations of national policy in a way that the Board is not." (Report, April 1958, para. 85.)

hand, the growth decisions of the industry should be influenced by more long-term policies than a single party in power could envisage. It is for this reason that, even while insisting on a ministerial direction on every intervention, one has to bear in mind the fundamental clash of interests that would arise between the Minister and the Board. In practice, however, the clash may be moderated by two factors, viz., that the Board's argument with the Minister would be taken up by the Opposition with sufficient force to prevent him from ignoring its content and that, in a vigilant democracy as in Britain, the Minister does not rush to pursue policies on which Parliament may be nearly equally divided.

We may refer to an important aspect of the "power argument" at this stage. The corporation method avoids the over-concentration of power with the Minister, as it provides the Board with the conditions of autonomous behaviour, within set objectives and rules. The Board might, if at all, abuse its powers to a limited extent and is always under the fear of criticism. If, on the other hand, the Minister has extensive powers of control, he could exercise them with an air of authority even if such exercise was prompted by political motives. Further, concentration in the Ministers of powers of control over many corporations has politically more dangerous consequences than limited powers remaining with individual Boards. In fact, the corporation is an important means of moderating the weakness of economic planning, viz., over-centralization of powers of decision.

Four important conclusions follow from the discussion. In the first place, the rationale of government control needs a thorough analysis, putting to test the simple plea that the Government, being the owner, must have control. The question is not one of "control or no control"; it relates to the purpose, extent and method of control; and when the emphasis is on the successful performance of the corporation, it is perhaps desirable that the Government's concern should show itself in setting up independent machinery for ensuring the efficient working of the Board. In other words, the case for control is tempered, and rightly so, by the inception of alternative machinery.

Secondly, the over-all objectives must be statutorily expressed and non-commercial responsibilities removed from the direct statutory duties of the Board. Statutory guidance must be given as regards broadly classified circumstances eligible to the special treatment approved by Parliament. Individual needs must be met by ministerial directions. Thorough—though not exhaustive—arrangements on these lines would keep the Board objectively accountable to the Minister, keep the Minister sufficiently accountable to Parliament and ease the controversy on government control.

Thirdly, all external decisions have their own consequences on the

Board's results.[1] If the Board is to be adjudged properly and if the public should have a fair idea of the cost of social or governmental policies—if, for example, we should know how far a certain price or price structure is employed to do the work of the tax and the budget—there must be periodical assessment of such consequences. The assessment is a difficult one;[2] and except in easily separable circumstances, we may not be able accurately to establish the causal relationships of external influences, as against the Board's own decisions, with the ensuing results; and there would be attempts by both sides—the Board and the Minister—to minimize their respective responsibilities for the consequences. (The "Clow differential" of 1948 may be cited as an example.)[3] Yet it is an inevitable task, if the problems of the corporations should not get too complicated. To give one illustration, it already seems difficult to know to what extent the financial condition of the London Transport Executive is due to its own commercial decisions and to what extent it is the product of government influence. The assessors must be an independent body,

---

[1] Margaret Finnegan observes, with reference to the Electricité de France, "A typical example, and one which caused very much disappointment in E.d.F., was the forcing down, in favour of thermal stations, of the percentage of hydro-electric stations in the provision of the total supply of electricity needed—a change of policy which was effected against the strongest wishes of the E.d.F." "The government's tariff-fixing policy can, and does, upset E.d.F.'s own tariff plans, and even their revenue estimates." In 1953 the Government ordered a cut by 5% in "the key components of the cost-of-living index", affecting electricity tariffs without warning. (*Public Administration*, p. 447.)

[2] Herbert Morrison observed, "it would need the wisdom of Solomon to disentangle the losses which were, in fact, due to such intervention from those which were due to other causes—such as inefficiency—or which might have been incurred if the Board had taken its own line, and to offset against those losses such profits as might have been due to other instances of government intervention." (*Public Administration*, Spring 1950, p. 5.)

A. T. K. Grant, in his evidence to the Select Committee on Nationalized Industries in 1957, suggested that, before a policy decision affecting the outcome of the trading accounts of the Board was made politically, the exact consequences of the decision—e.g., "such-and-such a loss"—were not worked out. (Q. 97.)

Section 34 of the Air Corporations Act, 1953, of India, provides for the Government reimbursing the corporations to the extent of loss relatable to the operation of a service conducted on government direction.

[3] The Committee to study the electricity peak load problem in relation to non-industrial consumers, recommended higher winter rates and lower summer rates. The Minister "wished the recommendations of the Committee to be implemented", though the Central Authority and the Area Boards "were most reluctant to implement the proposed differential charge". (The British Electricity Authority's First Report, p. 69.) The differential was then introduced. Consequent on their further representations, the Minister announced in Parliament that "it was not proposed to ask the Authority and the Area Boards to continue it in the winter of 1949–50". (The First Report, p. 70.)

assisted by the Department and the Board, and must be free from political influence. There may be one body of assessors for a group of public enterprises. Its work would be greatly facilitated if the central organization for the nationalized industry is revised as suggested in Chapter IV.

Lastly, it is necessary to ensure that the Board's operations are in accordance with, and do not contain any elements working against, the social policies which the Government or Parliament intends to implement. The rules suggested above help in this to a great extent. It is nevertheless necessary to set up a body which, from time to time, shall carry out the limited task of examining the broader social implications of the Board's policies—e.g., the effect of its pricing decisions on the redistribution of incomes, the distribution of population, the location of industry, inter-industry adjustments and special interests like agricultural improvements. This body ought not to consider questions of efficiency or the reasons for the Board's decisions; it should only draw expert conclusions on the broader results of the Board's performance, without casting aspersions on the Board. It could function as a periodical means of interpreting the Board's past working to Parliament and interpreting Parliament's current and future intentions to the Board. The exponents of the theory of consistency between Government and government corporations and of inter-corporation co-ordination should be satisfied with an agency of this kind.

An inquiry of this nature may form part of the Morrisonian "seven-year Inquiry", if the latter is set up. The case for it is, however, independent of the latter kind of inquiry.

### 4. *An empirical survey*

Though the corporation method has been widely used in different countries, there is no uniformity in the status of the corporation *vis-à-vis* the Government all the world over. An empirical survey, if made with the purpose of deducing generalizations of principle, may indeed be confusing and unhelpful at the outset. However, one must recall that the institution is still in its early stages of evolution and, unlike the older ones, e.g., the joint stock company, calls for certain adjustments with political institutions. The imprecision in the objects of public enterprise, the inability to draft accurate legal provisions and the complications in the synthesis of major economic changes with the concepts of democracy, have all contributed to the dissimilarities in the corporation–government relationships in different countries. Experience suggests that the autonomy and purpose of the corporation is qualified by six major factors as enumerated below.

1. *The role of the public enterprise in the national economy.* It is in countries where the public sector is of significance that an attempt is made to preserve the autonomous working of the corporation, to avoid the impact of political attitudes on too wide an area of the economy. The trend of thought in the U.S.A., which is by and large restrictive of corporation autonomy,[1] has to be understood in this context. V. O. Key observes, with regard to the role of public enterprise in the U.S.A., that "a political battle has to be won for any activity, whether or not it is conducted through the corporate forms".[2] On the other hand, in Great Britain, where the public sector accounts for a significant section of industrial employment,[3] or in India where about 75 per cent of the industrial investment under the second plan[4] is in the public sector, the managerial objectivity in the working of government enterprises must be preserved with care and zeal.

2. *The choice of the corporation form.* Many corporations in the world have been the product of wrong choice, carrying on transactions which are not of the business-type based on cost and price considerations.

(i) Extraneous considerations like the impossibility of expanding direct public enterprise because of a statutory ceiling on public debt,

---

[1] See Harold Seidman's article "The theory of the autonomous government corporation: a critical appraisal", *Public Administration Review*, Spring 1952; Herman Pritchett's article "The paradox of the government corporation", Summer 1941; and Marshall E. Dimock's article "Government corporations: a focus of policy and administration", *American Political Science Review*, October and December 1949. Lilienthal and Marquis indicate, in their paper "The conduct of business enterprise by the Federal Government", *Harvard Law Review*, 4th February, 1941, that the scope of public enterprise in the U.S.A. is limited to enterprises to aid private business and promote activities socially desirable, unprofitable but socially essential activities, fields where private enterprise is unsatisfactory and activities incidental to government functions.

[2] F. M. Max, *Elements of Public Administration*, p. 259.

[3] Aneurin Bevan says, "as far as Britain is concerned State direction of our economy in one form or other has come to stay, and it might as well stay in a respectable fashion by a radical extension of public ownership." (*In Place of Fear*, p. 117.)

"The number of persons employed in the public sector of the economy as a whole increased by 50 per cent between 1945 and 1950, so that by the middle of 1950, 22½ per cent of the total number of persons in civil employment were in the public sector.... In mid-1955 the position was still approximately the same." (*Britain: An Official Handbook*, 1956 edition, p. 131.)

[4] The investment in the public sector on industry, power and railways, planned under the second plan is Rs. 2,017 crores as against Rs. 575 crores in the private sector. "It is inevitable that the public sector must grow not only absolutely but also relatively to the private sector." (*Approach to the Second Five Year Plan*, p. 23.)

forced some countries, e.g., Puerto Rico, to resort to the corporation form;[1] and there was no genuine intention of letting them run as commercial and autonomous enterprises.

(ii) The corporation form is conferred on the conduct of trans-actions requiring expedition, as in the U.S.A., where the Government intervened in the country's economy at many points during times of war and depression. Some of these purposes were temporary and the corporation appeared to be a suitable arrangement that could be "lopped off" without difficulty at any moment. It is when a public enterprise has come to stay that there is emphasis on its managerial individuality, as in the case of the Tennessee Valley Authority even in the U.S.A.

(iii) When some governmental function or a policy measure, generally, though not necessarily, of a temporary character is organized as a corporation, it is likely to work with little autonomy; for the main requisite is ministerial and parliamentary influence on the working out of the policy—e.g., help in the field of agricultural credit in the U.S.A.[2]

(iv) If the Government creates a multi-purpose project or a development corporation, i.e., one which develops various industries, there is a justifiable tendency for the Government to exercise great control over it, since its working involves several value judgements, not inside a given industry or part of it, but among different indus-tries, which it is for the Government to decide upon—e.g., the Industrial Development Corporation and the Mineral Resources Development Corporation of Burma.

(v) The routine use of the corporation form for a large number of enterprises of varying kinds and sizes has weakened the emphasis on autonomy and encouraged the urge for standardized methods of bringing all those enterprises under government control. A corpora-tion, which need not be a corporation, prejudices the autonomy prospects of the others that need to have it. It is in the U.S.A. that the largest number of corporations have been set up and it is exactly there that the theory of autonomy is on the wane—"rejected," as Seidman observes, "both by the President's Committee on Ad-ministrative Management and by the Hoover Commission."[3] The

---

[1] The Reports of Frank C. Milligan and H. R. Balls to the United Nations Seminar at Rangoon in 1954 show that about a third of the Crown corporations in Canada owe their corporation status merely to simplify litigation.

[2] Harold Seidman gives the example of how the Virgin Islands Corporation might attempt to industrialize the Islands while the Government might be con-centrating on training agricultural workers. (*Public Administration Review*, Spring 1952.)

[3] *Ibid.*, p. 95.

Canadian classification of crown corporations into three kinds, departmental, agency and proprietary, has the merit[1] of proving that activities which need not be given the corporation form have been organized in that way for some accidental or arbitrary reason; and to think of the departmental and the agency corporations as setting the theory of the corporation, which is really the proprietary type of corporation, is to do injustice to the whole idea of the corporation.

3. *Financial status.* Corporations which are not self-sufficient have lent themselves to government control,[2] though, as shown in earlier discussion, this is not inevitable. Examples are provided by Greece where "the public corporations are not considered as profit-making enterprises . . . and they find it very difficult to be self-supporting",[3] by France where government policy upsets the financial self-sufficiency of the corporations (e.g., the Electricité de France) and by the early provisions of the Air Corporations in Great Britain.

4. *Board constitution.* Two types of Board composition may be distinguished: one which automatically becomes a vehicle of government intervention and the other which offers propitious conditions for government intervention. The former is the case when Ministers, civil servants and Members of Parliament occupy positions on certain Boards, as in Greece, Burma, Canada and India.[4] The second situation arises partly from the principle of representation of interests on the Board, which lets in government control, as in France, through the heterogeneity of the Board's attitudes, and partly from the monolithic structure provided for an industry on the *de facto* principle of functional verticality, as in the case of the National Coal Board.[5] In both these cases, the Government may not have originally intended to exert undue control; but the conditions for such interference

[1] Departmental corporations are those that are responsible for the governmental purposes of administration, supervision and regulation; agency corporations for quasi-commercial operations like service, procurement and disposal; and proprietary corporations for the ordinary business-type transactions.

[2] E. Davies observes, "financial autonomy of the public corporation disappears when it turns to the State for assistance." (*National Enterprise*, p. 148.)

The evidence of A. T. K. Grant, an Under-Secretary in the Treasury, before the Select Committee on Nationalized Industries in 1957 suggests that the Treasury's control would be less extensive in the case of industries which did not go to the Treasury for finance. (Q. 50.)

[3] George D. Daskalakis, *Public Enterprise* (edited by A. H. Hanson), p. 235.

[4] With regard to Britain, the appointment of civil servants to Boards has been a subject of criticism and Gaitskell suggests "no more civil servants". (*Socialism and Nationalization*, p. 27.)

[5] See R. Vance Presthus's paper, "British Public Administration: The National Coal Board", *Public Administration Review*, Autumn 1953.

present themselves after the corporations commenced operations. It is possible that the direct amenability of the Board members to the Minister's intervention would weaken, if an appropriate appointing machinery is evolved.

5. *The purpose of the public enterprise.* In several countries, constant intervention takes place in the name of economic planning and the public interest to be subserved by public enterprises. With a better understanding of the implications underlying these issues and with the statutory revisions suggested above, the rationale of government relationships with the corporations can be placed on a sound footing.

6. *The governmental machinery.* It is said, with the example of the South American countries, that there is a premium on autonomy in countries with weak or corrupt governments[1]—an explanation which fails when applied to the U.K. Further, in countries where the personnel in the government departments is not and cannot be made strong and skilled enough for the running of the enterprises, there is an insistence on autonomous organization which permits of the willing acceptance of Board memberships by private businessmen. The dearth of personnel is in fact a limit to public enterprise; but where the latter is decided upon, the best arrangement would be the autonomous corporation.

The above survey indicates that it is difficult to formulate the theory of the public corporation without a full understanding of the circumstances surrounding the institution in each country at a given time.[2] At the same time we must work towards a general theory of the corporation of the most useful kind and suggest that, where it ill suits a particular enterprise, it ought to be organized differently than in corporation form.

It would be useful to note that, despite the ministerial powers under the post-war nationalization Acts, there is an obvious insistence on the autonomy of the corporations in Great Britain. Coming from a country whose experiments with public enterprise have much to learn from, it has to be understood in its full context. The factors

---

[1] Harold Seidman observes, "If there is a single underlying theme in the literature of corporate autonomy, it is distrust of government" (p. 90). "It is significant that the theory of autonomous government corporation has taken hold principally in those countries in which the central government is weak or unstable, or in which there is deep-seated distrust of government." (*Public Administration Review*, Spring 1952, p. 96.)

[2] The conclusion that with the Corporation Control Act "the government corporation can be said to have come of age in the United States" (Harold Seidman, *Public Administration Review*, Spring 1952, p. 94) must be understood only with reference to the circumstances of the country concerned.

that have contributed to the concept of autonomy seem to be the following.

(a) The approach to nationalization has been pragmatic and the needs of reorganizing an industry for the sake of improved efficiency[1] have subordinated several other and ideological prejudices that could have caused more governmental intervention. As far as the nationalization was caused upon grounds of efficiency, the requisite of autonomy gained emphasis and the first reaction was the desire to keep out political influence.[2]

(b) The public enterprises operated by the corporation method have been required statutorily to earn not less than is sufficient to meet all costs, including interest on the (sometimes high) compensation amounts and, in the case of some industries, avoid undue preference. There has ever since been a growing trend towards pricing related to costs, the Herbert Report being the most important recent document insisting on that line. Though criticism of this attitude is not lacking,[3] the developments in the field of public enterprise have, on the whole, been consistent with that principle—e.g., Area self-sufficiency under the Electricity Act of 1957. One may hope that the occasional influence felt by the Boards against price increases—e.g.,

---

[1] Hugh Gaitskell observes: "Thus in all these instances the crucial arguments for public ownership were either that it alone could carry through the structural changes needed to increase efficiency, or, if this change had already been carried through and central planning and co-ordination established, that it was necessary, in order to protect the public from the evils of private monopoly." (*Socialism and Nationalization*, p. 19.)

The general philosophy underlying the Board appointments further supports the "efficiency" motive of nationalization in Great Britain. For instance, Ernest Davies observed, "it was also decided, after full discussion at Party Conferences and Trades Union Congress, that members of the Boards should be appointed on grounds of their suitability for the job, rather than as representatives of different sectional interests." (*Problems of Public Ownership—a policy discussion pamphlet* (a Labour Party publication, 1952), p. 5.)

[2] Marshall E. Dimock observes, "The British are apparently not so doctrinaire as to think that economic enterprises must be run by the Civil Service simply because consistency throughout the Government seems to require it." (*The American Political Science Review*, December 1949, p. 1160.)

[3] Regarding the Herbert Committee's insistence on prices based on costs, A. H. Hanson says: "Its latter-day revival of the doctrine of the invisible hand . . . has a curiously anachronistic sound . . . To apply it generally to nationalized industries, as the Committee persistently hints might usefully be attempted, would be to ask for trouble." ("Electricity reviewed: the Herbert Report", *Public Administration*, Summer 1956.)

John Strachey criticizes the idea that socialization is aimed at improving the efficiency of the industry and contends: "To argue so would be to degrade the cause of socialism to the calculations of the cost accountant." ("The object of future nationalization", *Political Quarterly*, Jan.–March 1953, p. 73.)

the British Transport Commission in 1956[1] and the Electricity Boards of Scotland—attracts sufficient attention for setting the government relationship on a more formal level.

(c) The most vital difference from the American conditions lies in the realization that in Great Britain certain public enterprises have come to stay.[2] There is, however, serious concern for avoiding the dangers of State capitalism as reflected in departmental administration of extending proportions of the national economy while trying to remove the alleged evils of large private organizations. The public corporation seems to stand in an intermediate position and offers itself as a "third force" in the field of industrial organization. There is a wide acceptance of the corporation method among the different shades of political opinion in the country.[3]

(d) The internal political situation of Great Britain constitutes a unique guarantee of corporation autonomy. It is the Labour Party that is anxious to make the corporation an instrument of policy; but it cannot destroy the concept of autonomy which it greatly helped to develop. However, the Conservatives, who believe less in "planning", have been administering the corporations since 1951, with the result that a political brake was put on the possibility of the corporations being converted into significant policy media. Now that both the parties fully know of the extensive potentialities of government intervention, it is likely that automatic checks over each party would ensue from the vigilance of the other.

(e) Lastly, the ministerial and parliamentary traditions of Great Britain have been responsible, in no small measure, in allowing corporation autonomy to remain a practical ideal. A survey of the practices of Ministers and Parliaments in different countries in this regard convinces us of the importance of this factor.

## 5. *The Public Corporation in an Under-Developed Economy*

The public corporation has been widely employed in the under-developed countries as a form of organizing public enterprises. The

[1] The British Transport Commission applied in March 1956 for an increase in freight charges and fares. The Government felt "justified, in the national interest, in asking the Commission to take a course which would involve an exception to the general policy in regard to the nationalized industries' charges" (reflecting costs). (*Hansard*, Vol. 550, col. 827.)

[2] For example, Arthur Palmer observed during the parliamentary debate on Gas and Electricity Reports in November 1957, "I feel that both sides of the House have been very anxious today to assume that public ownership has come to stay in these industries." (*Hansard*, Vol. 578, col. 1107.)

[3] As G. N. Ostergaard observes, "one of the most striking features of the development of the public corporation between the wars is the fact that it was supported by all three of the major political parties." (*The Manchester School*, May 1954.)

progressive expansion in the public sector has rendered the question of organization important, though it is difficult to conclude that the question is approached rationally in the case of every activity. It may be inferred from experience that, while not every commercial enterprise is organized as a corporation, corporations themselves are subjected to varying degrees of government control, which are not always easy to justify on logical grounds. The concept of corporation autonomy is not given due recognition in many cases; and the impression is developed in some quarters that, in the circumstances of the under-developed countries, (corporation) "autonomy, at least for the present, is something of a will o' the wisp, whatever form or organization may be chosen to ensure it and however carefully this may be devised".[1] In view of the central role of the public enterprises in the economies of many of the under-developed countries and the impact of organization on their successful working, it is necessary to probe deeper and examine if this impression is justified. We shall take India for the purposes of illustrating the study.

The main question raised for discussion here is whether the autonomy of the public corporation in an under-developed country should be qualified by greater government control than takes place in an advanced economy like Great Britain. In other words, does the fact of under-development indicate any bias one way or the other on the question of government control? The basic assumption of course is that the area of public enterprise is large. It is only then that the answer is of significance.

By implication the discussion refers further to the way in which the public enterprises, whose number is large and whose relative significance in the country's economy is great, ought to be so organized that the best results of industrial organization may be realized. The concept of corporation autonomy, without reference to this aspect, would be of nominal importance. For, a Government may respect the requisite of corporation autonomy but run all the public enterprises departmentally; with the result that direct control does not touch any enterprise designated a corporation, while the public enterprises all come under it nevertheless. The present discussion is, therefore, built up really on the assumption that commercial public enterprises are by and large given the corporation form, and is devoted to the rationale of government control in the circumstances of a developing economy.

At the outset, it would be useful to give a brief account of governmental intervention with corporations, which is statutorily possible in India. Two points may be noted in this connection: firstly, the intervention is unique, not in being more extensive than, say, in

[1] A. H. Hanson, *Public Enterprise*, p. 413.

Britain, but in involving certain qualitative differences from the British situation; and secondly, the traditions of intervention are different. Thus it is possible that, under like provisions, the Indian Government practises a policy of rigid intervention, as may be gathered from the working of the Damodar Valley Corporation.[1] Certain important provisions empowering the government to control the corporations are enumerated below. These are over and above the usual provisions of ministerial appointment, dismissal and directions.

(i) Civil servants can be appointed—and are, in large numbers—to the Boards of the corporations. Certain Boards are formed partly on the principle of representation of interests—e.g., ten members of the National Co-operative Development and Warehousing Board "represent" the Central Government.

(ii) Most of the corporations are required to submit financial estimates for the ensuing year for government approval and, subject to minor exceptions, keep within those limits. These estimates, as in the case of the Damodar Valley Corporation, are to be laid before Parliament and State legislatures.

(iii) The creation of reserves and the amounts to be credited thereto depend, in many cases, on the Government's decisions.

(iv) There is provision in most of the Acts for the annual surpluses of the corporations to pass to the Government. In the case of road transport corporations, the (State) Government specifies the per-centages of net profits to be utilized for amenities to passengers, labour welfare and other purposes, the balance being made over to the (State) Government.

(v) The accounts are audited by the Comptroller and Auditor-General of India, or by an auditor appointed by the Government, or by two auditors of whom one is appointed by the Government (e.g., the Industrial Finance Corporation).

(vi) The auditors of certain corporations (e.g., the Industrial Finance Corporation and the Warehousing Corporations) may be required by the Government to report on the "adequacy of measures taken by the corporation for the protection of its shareholders and creditors" or to undertake "any other examination . . . if in its opinion the public interest so requires".

(vii) The Government may, as in the case of the road transport

[1] A. D. Gorwala observed in his *Report on the Efficient Conduct of State Enterprises*, "Soon, however, after the corporation came into existence, the autonomy of the corporation seems to have become the object of considerable dislike in some governmental circles. It would almost seem as if they had not quite realized how much power was being conceded" (p. 33). "All in all, if an example was needed of how not to treat an autonomous corporation, this instance furnishes it" (p. 34).

corporations, control a part of the corporation's undertaking by placing it under someone else.

Let us examine the arguments usually advanced in defence of these qualifications to corporation autonomy, accepting as our assumption that the country is under a system of economic planning—e.g., as India has been since 1951.

(a) The exigencies of planning may call for quick changes in the investment figures of corporations, in the timing of capital expenditures, in the placing of orders involving foreign exchange and in the targets of physical performance from time to time.

(b) The conditions determining the financial resources for the plan may require quick readjustments not only in resource allocation but in the surplus policies of the corporations; i.e., the role of corporation prices as a substitute for the budget and for public borrowing may have to vary from time to time. It is an extension of this argument that the Government may wish to divert the surpluses of one industry for the purposes of another.

(c) It is necessary to influence the output and pricing policies of the corporations so that regional inequalities as well as the inequalities among broadly distinguishable consumer groups are countered as far as possible. The need is particularly great in an under-developed economy of a large size, where Gunar Myrdal's finding with reference to Europe, that regional inequalities are higher in the poorer countries, applies with particular force.[1] It is natural that decisions in this context must be at the instance of Parliament and the power cannot be delegated to the corporation Board.

(d) Where a development corporation is set up, e.g., the Development Corporations of Burma, it clearly calls for governmental control, since its decisions contain planning elements that should logically be characteristic of a planning commission under Parliament's aegis.[2] The examples of the Industrial Finance Corporation

[1] Gunar Myrdal, *Economic Theory and Under-developed Countries*, p. 33.

[2] "In view of the width of their responsibilities, it is important to ensure that the operations of the corporation are not inconsistent with the policy of the Government. The number of matters which have to be submitted for government approval is therefore greater than for the boards, and in practice more decisions are taken at a high political level." (A. H. Hanson, *Public Enterprise*, p. 433.)

A recent example of corporation functions bordering on policy matters is in connection with the National Co-operative Development Warehousing Board of India. Section 9 of the Agricultural Produce (Development and Warehousing) Corporations Act, 1956, requires the Board "to plan and promote programmes for the production, processing, marketing, storage, warehousing, export and import, of agricultural produce through a co-operative society or a Warehousing Corporation" and empowers the Board to grant subsidies to State Governments to finance co-operative societies and plan and promote several programmes "through co-operative societies . . . for the development of agricultural produce".

and the National Industrial Development Corporation of India may be cited in this context. The former is potentially in a position to make inter-industry choices as well as choices as between unit sizes, while carrying out its function of offering loans to industrial undertakings;[1] and the latter (which is registered as a company) obviously makes inter-industry choices in discharging its duties of sponsoring a new industry or industrial establishment, negotiating with foreigners for equipment and skill, managing undertakings and selling them out in due course to private enterprise.

Some of these arguments have great force in practice. Yet they do not destroy our main theory of the public corporation in the sphere of autonomous working. The first contention is intrinsically a reflection on the efficacy of the planning techniques; and the consequences of defective planning ought really to permeate all the affected sectors of the economy. The fact that the corporation runs a public enterprise ought not to subject it to particular control by the Government. It should be touched by governmental restrictions on industrial programmes in the ordinary way in which any other industrial undertaking is.

The second argument can be met by stipulating the financial targets for the corporations and the ways in which surpluses are to be appropriated, on which almost all the Acts are clear, laying down that the surpluses shall pass to the Government. No further intervention is necessary. (Price changes of too short-run a character— e.g., every three months—are bad in themselves; if and where the Government does want them a direction would be effective.)

The implementation of social policy through the corporation's output and pricing policies is not incompatible with its autonomy, if appropriate rules are written into the Act, as suggested earlier, and directions issued in the residual cases.

The last ground is the strongest; and it may be justifiable to constitute the activity as a Departmental Board, analogous to the Indian Railway Board, with a revolving fund, a somewhat separate budget and sufficient operational autonomy. It may, on the same lines as the Planning Commission, work in respect of the entire economy, plan its major activities and set up independent corporations for given jobs—e.g., the industries decided upon. The non-corporation form of the National Development Corporation is in this sense a com-

---

[1] The purpose of the Corporation is to make "medium and long-term credits more readily available to industrial concerns in India, particularly in circumstances where normal banking accommodation is inappropriate or recourse to capital issues is impracticable". No wonder the Corporation was subjected to several lines of criticism, resulting in the appointment of a Committee of Inquiry in 1953.

mendable step,[1] provided the industries it sponsors are individually given an autonomous form. The error of autonomy for a corporation engaged in planning, besides operating, functions, is most prominently seen in countries like Chile where the activities of the Corporation de Fomento cover planning, raising of capital, conduct of industrial operations and the promotion of technical skill. Clearly its functions border on certain ministerial tasks.

It is felt by some that the circumstances of an under-developed country in the throes of planning may necessitate such an extensive use of ministerial directions that autonomy might remain an academic concept, breached by constant, though formal, directions. This is no doubt a reasonable practical comment. However, adherence to the autonomy concept would compel the Minister to think twice before he directs; and gradually his intervention becomes most rational as well as most amenable to parliamentary scrutiny.

Let us now turn to the positive arguments for preserving the autonomy of the public corporation in the circumstances of an under-developed economy.

(a) Experience shows that planning should be flexible, if it is to be successful and not lead to frustration. Unfortunately it develops a rigidity with the extension of the planning outlook far beyond the framing of broad policies and the setting in motion of the stimuli necessary for their fulfilment. Public enterprises have potentialities of aggravating such rigidity through an over-centralization of powers of decision not only at the level of policy but at the executive stages. The less autonomously they are organized, the more difficult it is to follow up and evaluate the results of planning; whereas the more autonomous the public enterprises, the less the errors of centralized decision-cum-action in the name of co-ordination. For a country which still lacks adequate industrial experience, public enterprises devoid of autonomy are in the nature of a blind alley in the long run; and it cannot be known whether the results that ensue were the only ones possible and how far they were the product of government control.

(b) In a large country like India, where the economic conditions vary greatly in different regions, regional political pressures on the working of a public enterprise must be kept out as far as possible, since they correspond to the respective political strengths of the different States, without reference either to the commercial working of the enterprise or the removal of regional inequalities. The corporation is the best means: and it can act without regional bias (apart from that conveyed by the Act and the ministerial directions). This

---

[1] Though it shares the defects of the company form for public enterprises, as worked out in India.

is of great significance in fostering the most desirable atmosphere in the field of regional needs and pressures within a federal structure.

(c) The choice of public enterprise in an under-developed economy is often the result of a desire for a more rapid development and of a different pattern of it than would be possible otherwise, rather than the product of long experience with private industry in the fields concerned. It is an experiment whose novelty is twofold: firstly, there is a sudden impetus to industrialization of an unprecedented order, and secondly, most of it is organized in the public sector. While these factors raise enough problems demanding concentrated attention, it would be futile to complicate them with politics by permitting governmental intervention in the working of the enterprise. And so long as the main rationale of public enterprise rests on pragmatic grounds and is non-doctrinaire, there is no reason why this complication should be courted. Further, intervention is an easy temptation in a new democracy where there is yet a confused understanding of the motives of public enterprise; and interventions tend to be cumulative and set a bad precedent in the working of the enterprises. It is, therefore, desirable, in the ultimate interests of attaining the planned development, to set aside the temporary political advantages of interference with the corporations.

(d) A strong case against tampering with the autonomy of the corporation can be made out if we turn to the practical question of managerial skill. In spite of all the marked need for economic growth and the will to plan for it, there is dearth of managerial skill—not only of technical personnel but of those that organize in the most appropriate way what the consumer wants. The want is particularly serious where new industries have to be sponsored and managed. While industrial development is partly a function of the skills that the country possesses or attracts from outside, the progress of public enterprises is further conditioned by another factor, viz., whether the domestic skills available would be sufficiently interested to flow in. If we set aside doctrinal and political prejudices that might stand in their way—e.g., Paul H. Appleby's sweeping remark that "the business world is far from an ideal place from which to derive administrators of public enterprise"[1]—it can be concluded that the availability of skills depends on the conditions under which they have to work. An autonomous corporation undoubtedly offers the best conditions; whereas governmental control and intervention may turn out to be the deciding factor against the immigration of foreign skills. For, foreign businessmen with prestige would not like to work in a situation where their performance is not amenable to objective assessment

[1] Paul H. Appleby, *ibid.*, p. 44.

and political capital could be made out of the results of their operations.[1]

(e) There is a political ground in support of corporation autonomy. If we assume, as in the case of India, that the country believes in democratic institutions, it must follow as a corollary that, in spite of rational reasons for the public sector, the public sector ought not to provide the conditions for an undue concentration of economic power in the hands of the Government. That would be a weakness of potential political disadvantage. The temptation to exercise the power for the political purposes of a party or, what is worse, of a powerful group of individuals, would mark the beginnings of economic totalitarianism, with all its unpredictable political consequences. Thus we face a fundamental question: Is the object of public enterprise in an under-developed country rapid economic progress, or is it to permit entry of undemocratic institutions? Surely the latter is not the goal in most countries.

In concluding the discussion it would be interesting to refer to the recent episode of the Life Insurance Corporation, for it has valuable lessons to offer in the context of Government–corporation relations in an under-developed economy as illustrated by India. The relevant facts, which provoked public criticism and led to the appointment of a Commission of Inquiry, were that (a) the corporation purchased shares of above one crore of rupees, at indefensibly high prices, directly from a businessman "who was suspected to be a law-breaker and possessed a doubtful financial reputation and whose antecedents were of a most questionable character;"[2]—and this was known to the Government; (b) the transaction was, without justification, not put before the statutory Investment Committee of the corporation, and "deviated from both the provisions of modified Section 27-A and the general rules of guidance" laid down by the Committee; (c) the central figure in the whole deal was the Principal Secretary of the Finance Department who had *formerly* been the Chairman of the Corporation; and the Chairman—an I.C.S. man who "did not have much experience of the Stock Exchange"—was "overawed by his senior colleagues in the service" and the Managing Director of the Corporation said that "when the Finance Secretary asked him to do something, they looked upon it as a directive from the Government"; (d) the Corporation's defence of the transaction was that it would

---

[1] It has further to be remembered that today "the general pressure of British and foreign demand on the supply of British managerial and technical staff is very severe—much more so than in the decade prior to 1939, and possibly more severe than at any time in the past century". (J. S. Fforde, *An International Trade in Managerial Skills*, p. 35.)

[2] This quotation and the following ones are from the Report of the Chagla Commission of Inquiry (February 1958).

stabilize the Calcutta Stock Exchange—a point disproved by the Commission of Inquiry; (e) the Deputy Finance Minister went on declaring in Parliament that "the investment policy of the Corporation was dictated by the Investment Committee of the Life Insurance Corporation, that the Government had no hand in the purchases from time to time", that the investment was "solely with a view to getting a return and making a safe investment"; that the shares were purchased "at an advantageous price", that "so far as he was concerned the Life Insurance Corporation was not interested either in the stock exchange or in the brokers"—unfortunately the events as narrated and interpreted by the Commission of Inquiry refuted every one of these pronouncements; (f) and the Finance Minister denied having approved of the deal while the Finance Secretary claimed that he had the approval, nothing being on record on either side, though the Commission of Inquiry concluded that "clearly there is acquiescence on the part of the Minister".

A few of the consequences have been that the Commission found no justification for the deal, its manner and haste; one gets the impression that the motives need a further probe; the Finance Minister on whom the Commission placed "the responsibility for actions done by his subordinates" resigned; and further departmental and police inquiries have been set up by the Government.

Apart from the motives or the errors of judgement underlying the transaction, there are the following points of interest for the theory of the public corporation.

(a) The Government interfered informally with the Corporation, leading to "*particular* investments" by the Corporation—an effect that was impossible even under a formal directive that the Government was empowered to give; for Section 21 does not entitle the Government to "direct the Corporation to buy shares of a particular concern or belonging to a particular concern".

(b) The Chairman and the Managing Director of the Corporation proceeded on the belief that the Finance Secretary's word was virtually a directive; and the Chairman "was not even aware of the regulation which made it incumbent that the (statutory) Investment Committee should be consulted".

(c) It is not on record to what extent the Finance Secretary's part in the transaction had the Finance Minister's approval. In fact the Minister's refusal to accept full responsibility for every action of the Secretary strongly indicates the desirability of keeping the Department's informal interference with the corporations, as against the Minister's formal directions, to a minimum.

(d) The Corporation's defence of stabilizing the Calcutta Stock Exchange not only proved factually illogical but raises the question of whether such an "extraneous" purpose was within the legitimate area of the Corporation's initiative. That it is unsafe to empower the Corporation to interpret the public interest itself and act on it as it deems fit, is proved by the fact that, on inquiry, this deal in no way served the public interest. If the Corporation is allowed to indulge in such transactions, the results would be positively against the public interest.

(e) A stage is reached in India's developments in the public sector, when the question of appointing civil servants as members or chairmen of the corporations deserves serious rethinking. Civil servants so appointed must be made to realize, without reservation, that their exclusive concern is with the corporations served and that they should not use their positions as a means, however indirectly, of success in their governmental career. What is more important, the inclusion of civil servants in the Boards ought not to be envisaged by the Government as an unwritten medium of government influence on the corporations. As we turn to the civil servants in the departments dealing with the corporations, it is equally important that their contacts should be formalized so as to avoid any unpleasant criticism by Parliament and the public. The need is to conserve the limited talent of the civil service for the best purposes, relieving it from avoidable stresses. As P. H. Appleby observes, "the point is that in Britain the public service has high standing with Parliament and the public. Here (in India) it stands high with the public, but Parliament tends to be carping, unappreciative and miserly." "What is needed here . . . is a heightened recognition of the utter dependence of Parliament upon Administration for any actual achievement of its own purposes;"[1] and this would be possible if, at least in so far as the public enterprises are concerned, the role of the civil servants is well defined and is guided by clear and objective criteria.

To sum up: The circumstances of an under-developed economy are so complicated that the State may have to decide on playing an elaborate role in the economic development of the country. This by itself does not invariably imply rigid government control over corporations any more than is practised in an advanced country. On the other hand, there is much to be gained by running the corporations as autonomous commercial undertakings. This again does not mean that the Government surrenders its powers of direction over the economy. Corporation autonomy is not incompatible with the Government's over-all plan as regards the use of the nation's resources, the setting of targets of output and the promotion of capital formation.

[1] P. H. Appleby, *op. cit.*, p. 46.

One may venture to opine that a Government which plans the economy would gain substantially by creating autonomous units to take charge of the individual parts of the planned economic development. If they look like islands in the spate of over-all government direction of the economy, they have undeniably their own long-term merits.

# CHAPTER II

# THE MANAGERIAL FUNCTION UNDER NATIONALIZATION

MANY of the problems of efficiency and public accountability under nationalization are related, directly or distantly, to the distinctive nature of the managerial function as applied to a nationalized industry. In describing it in general terms, we have to note that the managerial function is under the influence of two major factors, viz., the nature of organization chosen for the nationalized industry and the degree of unification of operations within the industry. On these two grounds there are great differences from one nationalized industry to another. The British Post Office, the National Coal Board and the Hindustan Shipyard of India are examples of departmental, corporation and company organizations; and their characteristics in the field of management are not identical. Again, the National Coal Board is a monolithic unit; the Gas Boards are regional units; the former Iron and Steel Corporation retained some of the autonomous features of each public company; and the Renault motor works in France is but one (government) company in a large industry. Naturally the managerial problems met in these cases are bound to be somewhat dissimilar.

The present discussion, however, attempts to refer to those special features by which the managerial function under nationalization is marked, though qualifications to the statement are admittedly necessary in particular circumstances of organization. Wherever the organizational status, e.g., a departmental enterprise, or a peculiarity of internal composition, e.g., iron and steel while under nationalization, seems to call for a specific qualification, it will be mentioned. A major exclusion from the discussion is nationalization that leaves out a significant part of the industry or touches just one or a few companies in an industry for any special reason.[1] There are few examples of this method yet; and in any case the managerial function in this case is not likely to be under the same influences as described here. The post-1945 nationalization measures of Great Britain form the staple background of the present discussion.

There has been a tendency to equate the problem of managing a nationalized industry with that of a large private organization.

---

[1] An interesting recent example is of Pignone, a machine tool firm in Italy which had to be nationalized because it was about to be closed down.

For example, Lord Citrine observed that "centralization is not a phenomenon of nationalized industry. It is an inescapable consequence of economic forces and is a common feature of large-scale organization of all kinds."[1] A sub-division of the corporation or industry into divisions, etc., makes the problems of size "less intractable", in his view. Similar observations are found in the Fleck Report and the Herbert Report.[2] Such statements amount to an oversimplification of the problem; for both nationalization and the corporation method inherently imply many vital qualifications to the concept of "sameness" in the managerial problem.

## 1. The evolution of size

Let us accept that the element of largeness is apparently common to a nationalized industry as well as a large private unit. There is this difference, however, that by and large the largeness in the latter case is evolved through a process of careful deliberation on grounds of managerial efficiency, though a few large units might violate this criterion. Let us ask ourselves why the largest private units are not far larger still. Legal difficulties are only a part of the explanation, e.g., the inability of local authority units to expand beyond their defined boundaries in the U.K., and the anti-trust laws in the United States. There is really the fear of undue growth. The risk of inviting nationalization as an easy means of monopoly control is only a part of such apprehension; in the main it is fear of introducing into the organization difficulties of co-ordination and impediments to smoothness in the relations of a compositely responsible group—in other words, the fear of poorer results either in monetary terms or in terms of social organization.

It is generally agreed that a unit ceases to expand after a certain point, which may vary with time, place and industry, though differences exist on the reasons for this phenomenon. If one employs E. A. G. Robinson's technique,[3] there is a managerial optimum for the integration of commercial transactions under a given unit of

[1] Lord Citrine, "Problems of nationalized industries", *Public Administration*, Winter 1951, p. 321.

[2] Report of the Advisory Committee on Organization, National Coal Board, and Report of the Committee of Inquiry into the Electricity Supply Industry. "Much the same problem faces all Boards who are put in charge of large amalgamations." (Fleck Report, p. 7.)

"The industry now, as in the past, is organized on a monopoly basis. Nationalization merely enlarged the areas of the monopolies and reduced their number." (Herbert Report, p. 9.)

[3] E. A. G. Robinson, *The Structure of the Competitive Industry*.

control; and beyond a point managerial diseconomies outweigh the economies, if any, in other directions. Even under P. W. S. Andrews's concept of "management scales", "managerial costs . . . change in a series of plateau, falling at first and then rising after a point, beyond which each will be higher than its predecessor"; and if his "rigid assumptions" of "single product" produced "in a single place" are dropped, the decline in managerial efficiency beyond a certain size seems highly probable.[1] We cannot be certain of the rate of decline, since management is a human resource whose potentialities cannot be rated as those of plant can be. New techniques would go some way in enabling it to cope with a larger area of transactions; but enough have never been discovered to facilitate unlimited expansion. (The holding company technique is generally a financial technique, allowing delegation to subsidiaries of operating and managerial decisions.) We ought to attach some value to the clear empirical fact that, in most industries, units refrain from expansion beyond a certain stage.

Among the managerial techniques that make larger sizes possible are those that add to the ease of delegation. Unfortunately there are a few functions which only management at the top can deal with. These are (i) co-ordination, (ii) policy decision, and (iii) responsibility for final results. It is the difficulty of successful delegation in these respects that sets the limits to the size of a firm.

The private manager is always anxious not to approach the point of "unmanageability" which arises when, in the words of P. Drucker, the undertaking "is spread out into so many different businesses that it no longer can establish a common citizenship for its managers, can no longer be managed as an entity, can no longer have common over-all objectives."[2] The three-tier system (Area, sub-Area and district) in the electricity supply industry, criticized by the Herbert Committee, is an example of the multiplicity of managerial levels. The management structure inside the National Coal Board seems to be even more confusing and the hierarchy more elaborate than ever before—e.g., the National Coal Board (the only statutory body), the Divisions, the Areas, and the collieries, besides the Division Advisory Committee and the National Advisory Committee, as recommended by the Fleck Committee.

It should not be overlooked, while drawing comparisons, that in the case of the private units managerial faculty considers itself as a given factor at any unit of time seeking the largest area of transactions that it could negotiate with economy and smoothness. As per Coase's analysis, no transaction is assumed by a unit, which could be

[1] P. W. S. Andrews, *Manufacturing Business*, pp. 134 and 142.
[2] P. F. Drucker, *The Practice of Management*, pp. 205–6.

conducted cheaper outside.[1] In the long run the managerial area of a unit—i.e., the area of unified decision, co-ordination and responsibility for results—is not much larger than is consistent with the tests of gradual expansion.

With the nationalized industries, however, the area of managerial control is given, as it were, statutorily; and "fit" managers must be found; whereas it is to find the proper area of control that the energies of private managerial faculty are bent. The contrast does not concern nationalization alone, which only implies the transfer of ownership and management to public hands, but it depends on the way in which the public corporation of a given size is set up. Further, being the product of a sudden measure, the corporation lacks the twofold advantage which gradual expansion might have, viz., the discovery of new managerial techniques at and prior to every stage of expansion, and adequate familiarity with the nature and magnitude of problems which the previous expansion has brought to light. It is from this angle that certain defects pointed out by the Fleck Committee are fundamental, e.g., that "the lack of people with experience in the planning and execution of large-scale schemes of reconstruction is putting a severe brake on the industry's progress".[2]

Sir Geoffrey (now Lord) Heyworth has thrown some light on the differences in the evolution of large private units and the corporations in his answers before the Select Committee of Nationalized Industries. The question was whether "there was difficulty in obtaining the services of the right kind of men" for the coal industry. He made it quite clear that "the Coal Board is something thrown together . . . all at once. . . . Nobody would ever make an experiment of that size at all, and consequently the new organization does not have the advantage of one which has grown bit by bit by having a tradition. . . . It is not as if you have a nucleus and then just added to it. . . . A nationalized industry which starts in the way the Coal Board did . . . does start with a tremendous handicap over an outside concern which has grown bit by bit." When an analogy was drawn between the "large number of factories" of the Unilever and the "large number of pits" of the National Coal Board, he did not think "the two things are parallel".[3]

Corporations of a given size involve the finding of the "right men". However, the problem of managerial "finds" has basically changed with the kind of corporations set up since 1945. The managers of the corporations, unlike their counterparts in large private units, have neither the personal satisfaction of having evolved the right size by

[1] R. H. Coase, "The Nature of the Firm", *Economica*, November 1937.
[2] The Fleck Report, para. 111.
[3] Report of the Select Committee on Nationalized Industries, 1953, p. 85.

themselves (or others) through conscious effort, nor the necessary familiarity with the problem of the super-sizes they are asked to manage.

In concluding this section, we may refer to two contentions in favour of the sizes of undertakings generally set up under nationalization: (a) that the large-scale organization is followed by technical (including marketing) economies, and (b) that these outweigh the possible managerial diseconomies. The soundness of these two arguments depends on the facts; the optimal nature or otherwise of a nationalized undertaking can be established only on the basis of all the relevant evidence. It is not suggested that every Board operating under the British Nationalization Acts is supra-optimal. However, a thorough evaluation of the economies that result from and really depend upon the creation of large-sized units is necessary. It is possible to suspect that the National Coal Board as a whole is not an optimum managerial unit and that some of the Electricity Area Boards are too big to be in the nature of optimum units.

The above discussion applies with greater force to the public enterprises managed departmentally. Here the tendency to treat the whole industry as a single financial and managerial unit is stronger. The British Post Office and the Indian Railways, both departmentally administered, are examples of nation-wide units, despite decentralization in certain fields of operations. Under the corporation method, on the other hand, it is sometimes possible, as in the case of gas and now of electricity, to establish several autonomous units (though there is no guarantee that none of them is supra-optimum in size). This possibility has, of course, not materialized in the case of transport and coal.

## 2. Industrial totality

The managerial function under nationalization is generally qualified by the fact that practically a whole industry is brought under a single managerial unit or is divided into a very few large parts. As a first step in the analysis, let us examine the situation in the field of private enterprise. Except in a few cases of total monopoly, it is analogous to Sargant Florence's description that "in capitalist industry the unit of government comes very low in the whole structural scheme, and the top of the structure is really an anarchy; under normal circumstances there is no one organizing the whole of the industry, telling each industry how much output there should be or what prices to charge".[1] "Anarchy" here stands for the impersonal forces of inter-action, or the market mechanism, subject to the

[1] P. S. Florence, *The Logic of British and American Industry*, p. 21.

conscious inter-relationships to which some or all the units may subscribe from time to time.

The other feature of organization in private industry is that many a unit, which, by some convention of classification, is supposed to belong to one industry, carries on operations which are part of another industry. In other words, the units cross inter-industry barriers and treat themselves as "maximization units",[1] bringing under one managerial control all those operations which it is most economical to integrate, formally or thoroughly; and often there might be no significant technical integration. Leake and Maizels[2] and the T.N.E.C.[3] have given sufficient evidence of this tendency in the U.K. and the U.S.A. respectively.

Of course the non-integrated units within an industry are not absolutely without any formal or informal inter-relations. The chief motive of inter-unit relationships is to assure for each an external economy which exceeds what internal economy it may derive, alternatively, by taking on all functions capable of integration. In other words, the benefit derived from inter-unit relationships is greater than what could be derived internally for a given cost; or a benefit resulting from inter-unit relationships costs less than when it is sought internally. Research, co-operative advertisement and labour training may be cited as some instances. The units generally do not work out an integration of their production function, except during temporary periods of slump or any other special difficulty. It might not include all the units of the industry concerned, particularly when the purposes are specific and partial. Further, there is a point beyond which it becomes uneconomic or inconvenient to depend on an external economy through inter-unit relationships; and the attempts of inter-unit government beyond that point lead to a breakdown of the integration itself. In short, private combinations are limited in coverage, purpose, tenure and effectiveness and work under the fear of public censure, e.g., under the Restrictive Trade Practices Act, 1956.

As against this background of industrial organization in the private sector, nationalization introduces three changes:

(a) It generally "throws together" all the units in an industry—e.g., the National Coal Board. Even if we grant that nationalization involves some all-industry planning, we have to examine the implications of setting up a formal apex unit for the purpose of conscious planning or management of the whole industry and consider the

---

[1] Triffin, *Monopolistic Competition and General Equilibrium Theory*.

[2] Leake and Maizels, "The Structure of British Industry", *Statistical Journal*, 1945.

[3] The Temporary National Economic Committee, United States, Monograph 27.

desirability of limiting its function to the expert and unbiased presentation of facts conducive to ministerial decisions of the most appropriate kind.[1]

(b) Nationalization, as practised so far, makes a definition of industry inevitable, for it covers a named industry—e.g., the iron and steel industry. Certain integrations get broken—e.g., electricity-cum-gas units; while certain like operations are left out of nationalization —e.g., private generation—and remain outside the conscious planning by the top Board of the nationalized industry.

(c) Under nationalization, operations that have normally been organized under different auspices are sometimes unified under a managerial apex. This may happen under the name of "co-ordination", involving the protection of certain operations at the expense of the others, as a result of deliberate external decision. The original British Transport Commission is the best example. In its own words, "it is the aim of the design that its various parts shall be separately discussed, identified and judged so far as may be necessary."[2] The 1953 Act contained a logical reversal in the concept of integration at external instance; there is a hint in the Chambers Report of the desirability of a further functional slimming of the British Transport Commission.[3]

The managers of the nationalized industries are charged with not only larger but different functions than under private enterprise, in three respects. Firstly, they are to co-ordinate all production and all selling within the industry and bring about a conscious adjustment between supply and demand. These are particularly heavy responsibilities in the case of a monolithic organization. Such integrated functioning cannot succeed unless the industry is broken up into the necessary number of optimum units and, what is more important, these are allowed to work as optimum managerial units. In other words, a sizeable proportion of the normal processes of industrial organization must be re-introduced.

Secondly, nationalization usually makes for a spatial integration of operations far larger than ever before, though the technique of regional corporations limits it to some extent. It is true that certain private organizations are themselves regionally very extensive; but the manager acts under the fear of potential public (monopoly) regulation; and in many cases the extent of his area falls short of the whole industry. The problem faced by the manager of the nationalized industry takes a complex shape if the industry operates under varying degrees of monopoly in the different regions, and the cost-

---

[1] For further discussion see Chapter IV.
[2] The First Report of the British Transport Commission, p. 41.
[3] Report of the Committee of Inquiry into London Transport.

demand relationship is heterogeneous. The inter-regional considera-
tions arising in the field of pricing call for rare managerial capacity.
It can be seen at once that most industries, the British Transport
Commission in particular, belong to this kind.

Further, many managerial decisions tend to border on policy of
the ministerial kind. Most inter-consumer subsidies belong to this
category; and the managers should be functioning all the time with
a sense of grave responsibility. (They are spared this handicap under
private enterprise; for however big the unit, competition places
eventual limits on the extent of cross-subsidizations; or, alternatively,
monopoly regulation may be invoked by the consuming public.)
Rural electrification illustrates the point. The grant of £250,000 to
the South Western Board from central funds was an inter-unit
managerial decision, on the understanding that "the industry as a
whole will contribute towards the costs" of a weak Board. But
the matter could easily be one of public policy; this is illustrated by
the Herbert Committee's opinion that "the cost of such policies
should fall on the national exchequer rather than on the consumer of
electricity".[1] The basic question is whether any arrangement is possible, whereby the manager knows at the time of each decision that,
after the event, public opinion will not view it as a fit subject for the
Minister. As long as this is not adequately ensured, Board decisions
could contain elements of ministerial policy.

Thirdly, there ensues an undue integration in the field of ideas and
innovation. The several parts of the industry begin to develop too
much of an outlook of acting on readily integrable lines, in the name
of "co-ordination"; and the components entering policy formulation
are of a "sheltered" nature insulated from market tests. As the
Herbert Committee observed, there are now "certain obstacles to
the initiation of unorthodox and experimental conceptions".[2]

The managerial difficulties experienced in the field of all-unit
government may be illustrated briefly from the Fleck, Herbert and
Chambers Reports.

(a) The planning of capital outlays becomes a complex issue when
the market tests of the expansion do not apply to each part or to the
whole of the industry. This seems to be adequately illustrated by the
Herbert Committee's observation that "the control today, either for
seeing that unnecessary projects are not undertaken or for ensuring
that value is received for money spent on necessary projects, is somewhat weak. . . . At no stage in its career will this project be considered
individually or in detail by any body of people who are responsible

[1] The Herbert Report, para. 367.
[2] *Ibid.*, para. 425.

for financing it."[1] According to the Fleck Committee on coal, "capital expenditure schemes submitted to Headquarters for approval are often in an unsatisfactory form. . . . In our opinion, major capital projects . . . do not get enough scrutiny there (Headquarters). With such large sums involved, the schemes should have the thorough sifting and testing to which they would be subjected by a commercial concern in private industry."[2]

The Chambers Committee have raised a more serious issue of principle, viz., that the integration of the London Transport Executive with the British Transport Commission must have prejudiced the right kind of approach to the question of capital expenditure in the field of London transport. "The feeling in the minds of the members of the London Transport Executive that ultimate financial responsibility rests with the British Transport Commission may have led to inadequate representations in such matters as the urgency and economic soundness of improving London road conditions and to a rigidity in attitude of the London Transport Executive in certain matters where capital expenditure might have yielded a substantial return."[3]

(b) Certain observations of the Fleck Committee illustrate the National Coal Board's difficulties in promoting efficiency at each of the lower levels: e.g., "enough imagination or discernment in working out 'tailor-made', 'not mass-produced', standards for each pit is not shown by the Divisions and Areas; 'the industry at large continues to lack true cost-consciousness'; in several important respects the Board's views had been disregarded;"[4] and so on.

(c) Both the Fleck and the Herbert Committees have remarked on the friction and improprieties in the field of internal organization —weak discipline inside the National Coal Board, the Central Electricity Authority's interference with Area Boards and undue control over the Divisional Controllers, etc.[5]

---

[1] The Herbert Report, para. 352.
[2] The Fleck Report, paras. 337, 440.
[3] The Chambers Report, para. 362.
[4] The Fleck Report, paras. 326–8, 350, 359.
[5] The Fleck Committee are "not satisfied that policies and decisions emanating from the Board's Headquarters are being properly carried out in the Divisions and Areas"; "there is an unwillingness of the topmost management—the National Coal Board themselves—to insist on their policies being carried out"; "weakness of this sort at the top soon communicates itself to all levels of management below and inevitably brings the top management into disrepute;" "the problem of remoteness still largely remains" (paras. 298, 300, 302, 305).
The Herbert Committee referred to the Central Electricity Authority's objection "even to the experimental substitution of a two-tier for a three-tier system without the approval of the Authority" and remarked that "this appears to us to be interference which the Area Boards are likely to resent and do in fact

These weaknesses basically are derived from the new concept of managerial responsibility for all-industry government and are on the whole independent of the abilities of the Board members. If a generalization is possible in this respect, it may be stated that these weaknesses would be proportional to the functions of active management retained in the hands of the top Boards. Further, there develops a general bias for more central planning than is good for the industry.[1] The danger is that planning becomes an interest in itself as, according to Lord Citrine, "the most highly qualified of the experts and specialists tend naturally to be found at the centre where policy and its execution is planned, and their services can most economically be employed."[2]

It may be relevant in this connection to cite the Chambers Committee's "natural question" whether there is anything now done by the British Transport Commission in relation to the London Transport Executive's undertaking which the London Transport Executive itself could not do equally well or better."[3]

A word in the end regarding the departmental organization. It is characterized by a greater unification of all the operations within the industry than the corporation method brings about. Further, Parliament constantly criticizes even an apparent symptom of lack of co-ordination and tends to promote keenness on the part of the managers for deliberate and meticulous planning and standardized practice.

### 3. The objectivity of managerial behaviour

Managerial behaviour is at its best if it is based on the utmost objectivity. Apart from clarity on the objects of the business,[4] there should be clarity in the decisional processes leading to their achievement. Most decisions are the results of choice among alternatives, each of which is based on certain values, so that in the end decision-making

---

resent, a resentment which tends to build up into resistance to the Central Authority in other matters" (para. 242). "There is a similar feeling on the part of some Divisional Controllers that they are not given as much power and responsibility in relation to the design and operation of power stations as they could with advantage exercise and discharge" (para. 239).

[1] Lord Citrine, "Nationalization presupposes planning and co-ordination of the industry as a whole." ("Problems of nationalized industries", *Public Administration*, Winter 1951, p. 321.)

[2] *Ibid.*, p. 321.

[3] The Chambers Report, para. 364.

[4] Dr. Luther Gulick says, "A clear statement of purpose universally understood is the outstanding guarantee of effective administration." (*Administrative Reflections from World War II.*)

C

involves some value judgements. Unless the basis of relative valuation of the alternatives is fairly clear, it is difficult to maintain that the final decision is the best—for we do not know how to judge it as the best; nor would one decision bear close similarity of purpose. to another since the criteria—i.e., the relative emphasis on different values—may have been different in the two cases.

There are three major factors that qualify the objectivity of managerial behaviour under nationalization: (a) the legislation, (b) the concept of accountability, and (c) the composition of the managerial Board. Let us discuss these with reference to the public corporations.

(a) Though the Acts may try to promote the objectivity (i) by specifying the purposes for which the Board should strive, (ii) by laying down the conditions under which it has to look to the Minister for certain value judgements underlying some decisions, and (iii) by mentioning where the Minister ought to intervene in the managerial functions of the Board, there is still lack of clarity in what the legislation provides and what it omits to provide.

The former defect—lack of clarity—may be illustrated by reference to some of the objects statutorily imposed on the Boards. The Coal Nationalization Act made the National Coal Board responsible for "securing the efficient development of the coal-mining industry; and making supplies of coal available, of such qualities and sizes, in such quantities and at such prices, *as may seem to them best calculated to further the public interest*". (Section 1 (1) (b).) The British Transport Commission had the "general duty" under the 1947 Act "so to exercise their power . . . as to provide, or secure or promote the provision of *an efficient, adequate, economical and properly integrated system* of public inland transport . . ." The 1953 Act calls for "*due regard to the needs of the public, agriculture, commerce and industry*". The Electricity Boards are to "secure, *so far as practicable*, the development, extension to rural areas and cheapening of supplies of electricity; *to avoid undue preference* in the provision of such supplies; and *to promote the simplification and standardization* of methods of charge for such supplies." (Section 1 (6).)

There is great scope for ministerial influence in regard to what the Acts omit to provide. In fact this has been greater than the influence through directives in the U.K. The list of matters "which have been decided by or clearly engage the responsibility of any Ministers" is elaborate and extensive.[1] In fact, referring to his ministerial experience, G. Strauss said, "there was not a subject with which I was not concerned."[2] Under these conditions, what is the

[1] Special Report from the Select Committee on Nationalized Industries, 1955.
[2] *Ibid.*, p. 36.

extent of objectivity left to managerial behaviour? As D. N. Chester questions, "are not the present Boards being brought nearer to being departmental agencies, and is this what Whitehall and Parliament wants, or is the whole thing getting in rather a muddle?"[1]

(b) The concept of accountability, as derived from the general discussions on the issue, can at a certain stage clash with the concept of efficiency. The corporation lies midway between the department whose accountability is axiomatic and the private company whose eye is essentially on efficiency; it has to satisfy both the canons. For example, on grounds of efficiency the National Coal Board ought to follow a "vigorous policy" of retiring incompetent people,[2] and the Electricity Boards must "face" the problem of redundancy,[3] though the Boards seem to be afraid of doing so on grounds of public criticism. As long as the criteria and the media of judgement over the Boards are not clear, "the real danger to efficiency . . . arises", in the words of Sir Hubert Houldsworth, ". . . from the limelight of public criticism under which the work has to be carried out. . . . If a person fears such criticism he will be inclined to play safe instead of exhibiting that enterprise and daring which are so necessary for progress."[4] Obviously some of the media, e.g., Committees of Inquiry, create this atmosphere.

(c) Certain kinds of Board composition adversely affect homogeneous managerial behaviour—e.g., Boards formed on the principle of direct representation of partisan interests. France has adopted this principle with results that could only be expected. Incidentally, with such a method the Minister's position of control improves. More fundamentally there are three features of Board composition that qualify the element of homogeneity in its behaviour: (i) where the Board is composed of some functional and some non-functional men, between whose attitudes differences could arise; (ii) where the Board comprises full-time men drawn from within the industry and part-time men from outside, with perhaps different degrees of intimate knowledge about the industry; and (iii) where a Board is partly overlapped by members of other Boards having their own interests, resulting in occasional conflict of loyalties, e.g., the former Central Electricity Authority. Though private organizations are not free from these problems, they have the advantage of flexible solutions in given situations; whereas in the case of the corporation Boards an

---

[1] D. N. Chester, "The Select Committee on the Nationalized Industries", *Public Administration*, Spring 1956, p. 95.

[2] The Fleck Report, para. 118.

[3] The Herbert Report, paras. 270–1.

[4] Sir H. Houldsworth, *Efficiency in nationalized industries*.

elaborate case has to be made out for a change in Board composition and the Minister has to decide to act on it promptly. In any case decisions touching on Board membership could excite political criticism; and sometimes the statutory provisions governing the Board composition may operate too rigidly against the changes being brought about.

Of the three factors qualifying managerial behaviour—viz., legislation, public accountability and Board composition—the last one is the least important; for it is always possible for one or a few of the Board members possessing the necessary qualities of drive, if not domination, to bring about the desirable degree of homogeneity in the Board's decisions. The other two are the more fundamental limitations which the Board members, however able, cannot remove.

These conclusions apply equally to the company form of public enterprise. With regard to the departmental type of organization, however, the problems seem to be simpler. For the civil servants manage the industry according to the parliamentary appropriations, displaying far less of initiative than the corporation Boards and depending on the Minister for clarification or direction in any situation of doubt. In any case the responsibility for their actions is constitutionally borne by the Minister, with the result that, on the one side, the Ministers are careful to see that the civil servants so behave that they (Ministers) would not find it difficult to be answerable for their actions and that, on the other side, the civil servants themselves take care not to behave in such a manner that might provoke disciplinary action on grounds of transgression of set rules of behaviour. To put it briefly, the managerial function mainly rests in Parliament and the Ministers; and it is understood that the managerial role of the civil servants is severely circumscribed by the criteria and priorities constantly set by them.

## 4. *The setting for managerial evolution*

Let us now consider the question most relevant to the growth of the industry, viz., the evolution of managerial talent over time. The normal process under private enterprise is for a person to be in independent command of successively bigger units, so that he gradually gains the experience necessary for the management of the large unit. Independent command enables one freely to experiment with new ideas; and he has only "to turn up at the end of the year with having made slightly more right guesses than wrong guesses".[1]

---

[1] Sir Geoffrey (now Lord) Heyworth's answer to Q. 689 of the Select Committee on Nationalized Industries, 1953.

It is true that many top managers have grown inside given units;[1] but their growth within the organization is distinguished by two conditions, viz., that it is openly or impliedly subject to the competitive tests imposed by outsiders seeking to come in, and that their growth from stage to stage is not a function of time or seniority but depends on the results of performance for which they are responsible.

Let us look at the dissimilarities in managerial evolution under nationalization. The primary complication is that persons who have been in functional charge find themselves promoted to higher levels where less of functional expertise and more of over-all policy-making talents are required. Though private organizations are not free from this problem,[2] the position is worse with public enterprise, for (i) the appointment of "outsiders" becomes exceptional in course of time and (ii) the insiders grow in an environment where they do not have the privilege or experience of the real managerial functions of making decisions and taking responsibility. If, due to habit, the promoted men tend to practise functional control over the lower levels, not only does friction develop in the organization but, what is more important, the managerial growth of the men below is heavily prejudiced. The process might well be cumulative.

The second qualification to the managerial growth is that the intermediate levels have no objective financial criteria to satisfy or be judged by. This is basically due to the "over-all" financial provisions contained in most Acts.[3] The Gas and Electricity Boards are by way of being an exception, though what is required in the present context is the demarcation of regions smaller than the Gas or Electricity Areas as the managerial units with specific financial targets. The demarcation need not necessarily be statutory. The Herbert Committee conceived "genuine management districts" under

---

[1] For example, the average service with the company before appointment as Director was as follows in some of the biggest companies:

| | |
|---|---|
| Imperial Chemical Industries Ltd. | 25 years |
| Unilever Ltd. | 20.5 ,, |
| Courtaulds Ltd. | 11 ,, |
| Dunlop Rubber Co. Ltd. | 22 ,, |
| Associated Electrical Industries Ltd. | 27 ,, |
| General Electric Co. Ltd. | 26.6 ,, |
| Associated Portland Cement Manufacturers Ltd. | 13.5 ,, |

(Lord Simon of Wythenshawe, *The Boards of Nationalized Industries*, p. 16.)

[2] Myles L. Mace, *The Growth and Development of Executives*, pp. 9–10.

[3] These are the provisions requiring a nationalized industry to earn not less than is sufficient to cover costs, taking *all* the operations as a single unit. For example, Section 1 (4) of the Coal Industry Nationalization Act, 1946, lays down that "the revenues of the Board shall not be less than sufficient for meeting all their outgoings properly chargeable to revenue account on an average of good and bad years".

the Area Boards and recommended "as many" of them "as possible". It is, however, doubtful how genuine they could be in offering the district manager propitious conditions for measurable efficiency, in the absence of even a rough balance sheet of his efficiency. The Board's practical objections could be met by a system of pricing for the units (districts) the services that have to be centrally provided in the interests of specialization and economy. Unfortunately the Herbert Committee did not go further in recommending a workable framework of regional assessment.[1] With regard to the coal industry, whose managerial and financial centralization is statutory, the Fleck Committee expressed themselves unequivocally against the concept of regional financial criteria.[2]

The regionalization of financial responsibility, as far as possible, would encourage the top Boards to delegate certain powers whose exercise is a necessary part of managerial growth at the lower levels; and there would be less room for the Boards to contend, as Lord Citrine did, that "if responsibility for the conduct of an industry is placed upon a central body, there are obviously limits to the extent to which it can delegate the responsibility without fear of incurring undesirable and serious consequences".[3] The top Boards have been so constituted that there is an unfortunate tendency to think in terms of what functions, and how many of them, should be given to the lower levels of management rather than what functions, and how few of them, should be taken over at the apex. Lord Citrine visualized decentralization "without impairing the efficiency of the industry and the responsibilities of the central body",[4] whereas the attitude ought really to be one of such minimum centralization as would not impair the efficiency of the individual units of the industry.

Thirdly, the methods of managerial training become complicated under nationalization. One of the fundamental problems, to which the Herbert Committee referred, is the lack of "selective training". The Boards inherently proceed under the fear of public criticism of invidious selection and nepotism, of which political capital could be made. Thus a good practice of private enterprise does not work equally well within nationalized industry; for the Boards would sooner prefer not to rouse criticism than to raise good managers. A Selection Committee, not exclusively composed of Board members, might be a helpful development in this direction. The point is far-reaching indeed, in that the more purposive the Board's own selective training

[1] The Herbert Report, paras. 143, 295, 297.
[2] The Fleck Report, para. 184.
[3] Lord Citrine, "Problems of nationalized industries", *Public Administration*, Winter 1951, p. 321.
[4] *Ibid.*, p. 323.

the narrower the Minister's choice for top appointments to the Board in course of time.

These remarks are not a plea against training; their purpose is to show how a normal practice of private enterprise becomes complicated under nationalization. Further, however valuable training may be, it cannot be a substitute for experience in conditions requiring initiative. It would be desirable to explore the possibility of providing opportunities for the middle level of managers to work in outside enterprises for a period, so that they develop in a wider, uninhibited managerial environment.

The above argument relates essentially to the corporation type of public enterprise. A departmentally organized enterprise offers obviously inferior conditions for the development of managerial talent. In fact it is on this ground that the case for a corporation is often built up, on the assumption that the corporation is free from the personnel rules and routine characteristics of the departments. To many corporations, as in Greece, however, such departmental procedures are fully applied; and certain corporations, as in France, are under governmental influence with regard to recruitment, e.g., preferential treatment to war victims under an Act of 1946; so that the environment in which managerial growth takes place is really less favourable than ought to prevail under the corporation method.

Where the organization most resembles that of private enterprise and where, subject to the establishment a central organization for purposes of policy formulation, supervision of the nationalized industry is substantially preserved, the conditions under which managers develop are bound to be favourable. The Iron and Steel organization, during the brief spell of nationalization, is the nearest example to cite in this connection. Without prejudice to the fact that the Iron and Steel Corporation was in the nature of a managerial body, it can be maintained that the non-disturbance of company individuality in some respects preserved some of the ordinary processes of managerial evolution. It is difficult to say, in view of the short experience (shrouded, further, by political uncertainties as regards that measure of nationalization), whether the conditions would have remained the same in course of time and whether the central organization might not have had a restrictive influence on the managerial initiative at the company level.

## 5. Conclusion

The above analysis brings out the basically distinctive characteristics of the managerial function under nationalization, though identically similar arrangements are not inherent in every scheme of nationalization. A few suggestions may be made to deal with the handicaps introduced by nationalization in the field of management. Some of these are elaborately discussed elsewhere in the book.

(a) Some rough, regional, financial criteria should be set up—a region to stand for a smaller area than the (Electricity or Gas) Area, in many cases; and the top Boards should function in a far less managerial capacity than at present. One of their most important functions should be the working out of regional financial criteria and comparison of regional results.

(b) It would be desirable to promote—or err on the side of—far more competitive "aberrations" on the part of the constituents making up the industry and relax substantially what might tend to be a professional planning interest at the apex.

(c) It would be appropriate to limit the Minister's effective contact with the corporations to a few points in their working. The public should know of every contact made; and the consequences on the Board's performance and finances should be assessed, though roughly.

(d) It would be inevitable in course of time to devise a well-defined system of making top appointments, under which one who seeks advancement can act on specific criteria.

(e) It would be necessary to provide opportunities for the middle line of managers to gain outside experience.

# CHAPTER III

# PRICING AND POLICY:
## A CASE STUDY OF ELECTRICITY

It is generally believed that the corporation method ensures that all commercial decisions are autonomously taken by the Board while decisions involving broader national interests or issues of social policy are reserved for the Minister or Parliament. This is indeed a simple basis for the demarcation of decisions. In practice, however, the statutory arrangements do not seem to maintain the spirit of this basis to any significant extent. The present case study of the electricity supply industry is intended to illustrate that certain decisions of the Boards in the field of pricing do border on "policy" which is really a ministerial or parliamentary prerogative. It will be followed by a few suggestions designed to show more clearly than under the present Acts the decisional areas of the Boards and the Minister respectively.

## 1. *"Policy" implications of pricing*

There is little doubt that, where social and commercial purposes are mixed in the definition of the corporation's responsibilities, the Board's decisions contain elements of general policy. Section 2 of the Hydro-Electric Development (Scotland) Act of 1943 is an obvious instance, requiring the Board to "collaborate in the carrying out of any measures for the economic development and social improvement of the North of Scotland District or any part thereof". Section 1 (6) of the Electricity Act of 1947, which imposes on the Electricity Boards the duty to "secure, as far as practicable, the development, extension to rural areas and cheapening of supplies of electricity", has a somewhat similar influence on their working.

The more important cause of commercial decisions being mixed with policy matters is the large size of the corporation, which is permitted by the financial provisions of the Act to operate a variety of discriminatory price structures. The statute does not compel the corporation to base its price structure on cost considerations alone; and the alleged difficulties of appropriate cost break-down offer the Board an opportunity to approach its pricing and development problems from the "aggregate" or over-all angle.

Before we proceed further, the connotation of the term "policy" as employed in the present discussion may be noted. It is meant to convey that element in a particular price, a price structure or price level whose main justification is not derived from internal criteria of cost. In other words, policy elements are contained in price fixation, which results in indeterminate surpluses and in price discriminations which either cannot be adjudged—due to the dearth of the requisite cost data—or cannot be supported by cost differentials where these are known. The ability to maintain the discriminations is derived from two conditions: (a) the corporation has enough monopoly in the high-demand areas to ignore the prospect of competitive pricing at cost level by any other undertaking; and (b) the corporation is sufficiently large to shift its advantage in a region or with a consumer group to the relief of another region or group. It is not necessary that decisions involving such discriminations should be the exclusive responsibility of the Board; for value judgements of the kind that call for ministerial or parliamentary decisions underlie such decisions in the ultimate analysis.

The best way of understanding the "policy" opportunities open to a Board is by analysing the principal financial Section 13 of the Electricity Act, 1957: "It shall be the duty of the Generating Board and of each of the Area Boards so to perform their functions as to secure that the revenues of the Board are not less than sufficient to meet the outgoings of the Board properly chargeable to revenue account, taking one year with another." Though this has, on the whole, the effect of limiting the pricing considerations of a Board to its own Area and resources, unlike the 1947-Section 36, it gives room for any of the following possibilities in practice; and every one of them involves considerations that ought mainly to fall within the purview of the Minister and Parliament.

(a) As Section 13 lays down a minimum below which the Board's revenues must not fall, it allows the Board to realize an indeterminate surplus over and above the interest charges and contributions under the Electricity Council's directions. Even if a policy of profit maximization is suspect in the case of the nationalized industry,[1] the Board is free to collect from the consumers an indeterminate excess over cost—the extreme limits being zero surplus on the one side and the theoretical profit-maximum on the other. It is doubtful whether the exact amount collected—and this may vary from year to year—ought to remain a matter for purely internal decision, once a reason-

---

[1] S. Silverman observed during the debate on the Gas and Electricity Reports in the House of Commons on 26th November, 1957: "In so far as a profit is made over and above having provided for all those things (costs), the consumer is being charged too much. That is all very well for a private business. . . . But it is not the business of a nationalized industry which is trying to run a part of the national wealth in the interests of the community as a whole." (*Hansard*, Vol. 578, cols. 1070–1.)

able reserve for business reasons is built up; and it is the Minister or Parliament that should really decide the issue. Yet under the Act the Board can be the arbiter in this regard.

(b) Slight variations of the above situation are those where the Board can choose, either through indifference or by positive preference, a particular scale of output from among a variety of alternatives, all leading to the same surplus. It is in cases such as these that the choice of means (in attaining a given financial result) assumes importance from the public point of view, especially where it is in the spirit of nationalization to maximize output consistent with adopted financial criteria. Wherever, with a little effort, the Board discovers as alternatives two levels of output that lead to the same result, let us assume that it chooses in favour of the higher output. Unfortunately, under the Act it is not obliged to explore alternative means of action. Further, there are the more frequent occasions when different alternatives are likely to be followed by different surpluses. If the Board chooses the most profitable course, that would at least be understandable; whereas any other choice is bound to involve obvious preferences among regions or consumer groups, without any particular justification. As the Board is not provided with helpful rules of guidance in effecting a choice among alternative surpluses, the Board cannot be condemned for its actions; but at the same time value judgements are admitted.

The price structure—as against a ruling price level—is of great significance in the public utility industries like electricity, whose customers can be classified on grounds of region, use of product, time of consumption and ability to pay. Though it may be impossible to effect an atomistic allocation of all recoverable costs, unit by unit, it is necessary to allocate costs between consumer groups and between regions far smaller than the Areas. Some consumers—e.g., those who can generate their own power—enjoy protection against excessive prices; but the others do not; and some groups tend to pay relatively more than others. This gives rise to cross-subsidization; the Board ought not to be the arbiter of it, though in fact it is, in the absence of provision for challenge either under the Act or by consumer interest.[1]

Let us turn to rural electrification for an illustration. The question broadly is: to what extent should the Board go in undertaking high-cost electrification in the sense of revenues not being able to cover the costs? Clearly the Act has no answer except in terms like "as far as practicable"; and the Board has to find its own answers to several questions. For example, how far should the Board go in the direction of high-cost programmes, if it maintains uniform tariffs? Is it possible

---

[1] The consumer councils are unable to present effective challenge in this respect.

or desirable to fix high prices that fully reflect the related high costs? To what extent may aggregate profitability of the Board be allowed to fall in the interests of such expansion? (The break-even concept is not set by statute as a criterion to guide the Board.) Is it desirable to finance the high-cost programmes by effecting price increases in general; and should any such increases be uniform over all prices or discriminatory within the price structure? If the latter method is preferred, how exactly should the Board proceed in working out the new price differentials among the different consumer groups? Is it to be guided only by its monopoly power in the respective markets and is it possible to verify whether it exercises its monopoly power at random? The fundamental issue underlying these questions is that a high-cost programme, not followed by high enough prices in the corresponding area, has the effect of restricting consumption in the other areas by raising prices there or of preventing them from falling. Further it promotes a deliberate spatial shift in the use of factors, a shift that calls for governmental or Parliamentary approval as it requires judgements about human welfare.

It is not surprising that the indeterminate possibilities of high-cost electrification under the Act have encouraged much varied criticism. (i) The most common criticism is that the urban areas are paying too high prices.[1] This raises the broader question of whether the nature

---

[1] For example, W. A. Wilkins mentioned in Parliament: "it is true that even the South-West region . . . has this year again made a surplus. It has, however, been made very largely at the expense of people in the City of Bristol which happens to be the only industrial centre in the whole of the region. A terrific burden has had to be placed upon a population which, prior to nationalization, enjoyed almost the cheapest electricity supply in the country." (*Hansard*, Vol. 578, col. 1058.)

D. L. Munby observed in his memorandum to the Select Committee on Nationalized Industries that "it would seem wrong that the relatively small, and not very prosperous, industrial areas of Dundee and Aberdeen should bear an undue part of the cost". (Report from the Select Committee on Nationalized Industries, 1957, p. 187.)

The Committee's refutation of the criticism is unconvincing. That the tariffs in the North of Scotland Area are "by no means unduly high—they are, for instance, lower than those charged in Southern England" (p. ix), does not disprove the main point that the urban prices are higher than they could have been on the "related-cost basis"; that South Scotland, "if any one", is subsidizing rural electrification in North Scotland since "a large part of the Board's income is in any case derived from the sale of electricity to the South of Scotland", is equally unhelpful in disproving the basic criticism of cross-subsidization; and as Munby said, "nor would it be very desirable if the subsidy were paid by charging an uneconomic price for electricity supplied to the South of Scotland" (p. 187); and that under alternative methods of supply by "their own steam or diesel power stations", the towns "would have to pay more for their electricity than they do now" (p. ix) is beside the point of cross-subsidization under the given set of circumstances.

of a town's immediate or remote neighbourhood should prejudice its own conditions of cheap electricity. (ii) The Areas, as defined, are marked by varying degrees of responsibility for rural or high-cost electrification;[1] with the result that, if rural electrification is left as an exclusive responsibility of the Boards consistent with their finances, two results can follow—firstly, rural consumers in some Areas can never benefit equally with those in others; and secondly, the price levels and the price discriminations in the different Areas imply quite different cross-subsidizations among consumer or regional groups, i.e., there are varying transfers of benefits analogous to the working of taxes rather than prices. In strict theory, it is for Parliament to judge how to spread the burden of high-cost electrification among "able" consumer groups, wherever they lie in the country, over and above their payments towards costs related to their intake. The Select Committee's conclusion that the North of Scotland Hydro-Electric Board "is holding a just balance between demands of all its consumers"[2] could be a question-begging one. (iii) The burden of cross-subsidization is dependent on the organizational structure of the industry.

While the 1947 Act made national cross-subsidizations possible, as evidenced by the grant of £250,000 to the South Western Board from the central funds, the 1957 Act apparently limits these to the Area level.[3] If Area demarcations were different, a different pattern of shifts of benefit would arise; while the promotion of self-sufficiency below the level of the Board would confine the shifts to narrower limits.

(c) Tariff standardization, of which special mention is made in Section 1 (6) of the 1947 Act, can be another source of decisions which border on social policy. Though it mainly refers to tariff methods, there has been a tendency for some degree of uniform pricing as well. Uniform prices under conditions of varying costs are a medium of inter-consumer shifts of benefit. Support for uniform

---

[1] For instance, F. H. Hayman said that "there are still 43 per cent. of farms in the area (South-West) without electricity. To achieve the national average of 85 per cent., nearly 10,000 more farms will have to be connected. The increasing cost of connections is causing anxiety." (*Hansard*, Vol. 578, col. 1090.) R. Gower observed: "The progress of rural electrification in South Wales . . . is . . . rather less than that achieved in some other parts of the United Kingdom" (col. 1092).

[2] Select Committee Report, para. 26.

[3] W. A. Wilkins observed: "A terrific burden is still placed upon them (Wales, Cornwall and Devon) because the change of structure of these industries was designed to make them individually self-sufficient over the regions." (*Hansard*, Vol. 578, col. 1058.)

prices is voiced in Parliament from time to time.[1] A Board with a keen eye on uniform prices may tend to neglect certain high-cost programmes that turn out to be inconsistent with the single price level, though the consumers concerned might be willing fully to contribute towards the high costs. This is where insufficient attention to the consumer's willingness to pay cannot be justified in the context of expansion. A high-cost project which consumers are willing to remunerate through high enough prices tends to be placed, along with a high-cost and unremunerative project, in the category of projects not taken up.

(d) The length of the period over which the "not-less-than" concept should apply is far from clear. In the case of Boards with comfortable surpluses this is not an important matter at all. But Boards whose financial condition is marginal may find in Section 13 room for following policies whose commercial results are not immediate; and too much emphasis might be given to such social purposes as rural electrification and tariff standardization. In other words, over a period of time a variety of cross-subsidizations is possible.

The above account indicates the enormous powers of the Boards to touch on policy while carrying on their normal functions. It would be inaccurate to assume that the Minister has no power to intervene. Under Section 8, he can give "such directions of a general character . . . as appear to the Minister to be requisite in the national interest"; under Section 20, he can give directions (whether of a general or a specific character) as to "(a) any matter relating to the establishment or management of a fund which the Board are required to maintain under this section, or (b) the making of contributions to such a fund, or (c) the application of any moneys comprised in such a fund"; and under Section 22 he can give directions "as to the application of any such excess of revenues over outgoings" of the Board. However, these powers do not adequately help in preventing the Boards from decisions involving social policy. For (i) primarily these call for positive actions on the part of the Minister who may have to demonstrate the nature of social policy otherwise involved in the Board's own decisions; (ii) *ad hoc* directions directed against one course of action or in favour of another do not enjoy full political immunity; (iii) ministerial directions specifically affecting a course of action on the part of the Board may be criticized as incompatible with the Board's statutory financial responsibilities; (iv) piecemeal ministerial

---

[1] W. A. Wilkins remarked: "The ultimate aim of nationalized industries . . . was to provide a uniform and standardized tariff throughout the country. . . . These industries have now been in public hands for ten years and we hear even less talk today of standardized tariffs than we did before." (*Hansard*, Vol. 578, col. 1057.)

interventions in the Board's pricing and financial affairs would ordinarily result in removing all semblance of stable criteria of output and investment decisions. This is the gravest problem in the long run. We may find one Board building up huge reserves and using them for self-financing, while another may have to depend on capital issues for expansion. As the cost-price relationships vary enormously from Board to Board, we would soon lose inter-regional consistencies in the function of price as a guide to investment decisions and in the acceptance of the consumer's willingness to pay as an influence on output policies.

At this stage we may comment on the contention (a) that the pricing practices of some large private organizations contain policy elements mentioned in the present discussion and (b) that, as long as there is neither public challenge of them nor machinery to deal with them, it would be over-critical to raise the issue with reference to public enterprises. It is true that some large units practise price discriminations not supported by cost considerations. But the checks should come from competition which has the eventual effect of introducing rivals in the highly priced lines of business. Where competition is insufficient to bring it about, i.e., wherever competition is imperfect, resort may be had to monopoly regulation so as to prevent the private units from exploiting certain markets for the sake of either maximum profits or other markets. If the machinery of monopoly regulation has not been effectively used in this direction, it is because the question has not yet stimulated adequate recognition. The case of the public enterprises differs in that by and large they operate as monopolies not subject to specific monopoly regulation.

Moreover there is a fundamental change in the situation. Private units could work—they might not always do so—in the interests of maximum profit, adopting whatever policies remain unchecked by competition or public regulation. Whether the public enterprises are expected to work exactly on similar lines is a question which has not yet been answered by Parliament. In the unlikely event of bare profit maximization being outlined as the ideal of the public enterprises, those pricing decisions which contain policy or tax elements and lead to indeterminate surplus targets, should cause public discussion.

Public discussion on the policy and tax implications of the decisions of the corporations probably will be extended eventually to similar subjects concerning private enterprise. In course of time the question would seem to merit an answer without regard to the nature of the enterprise.[1]

[1] It seems very relevant to refer to the recent inquiry into the supply of certain industrial and medical gases conducted by the Monopolies and Restrictive Practices Commission. (Report published in December 1956.) The British Oxygen

## 2. *"Central" decisions*

Though the 1957 Act makes inter-Area shifts of benefit more diffi-cult than under the 1947 Act,[1] it does not render them wholly

Company holds a monopoly position in the supply of oxygen and dissolved acetylene. It accounted for more than 90% of these supplies in 1954. Among the Commission's findings, the following illustrate that certain questions of inter-consumer or inter-regional interest have begun to assume prominence in public discussions and would call for suitable policy decisions at governmental level.

(a) "In order to maintain and develop its business, a monopoly company in B.O.C.'s position does not . . . need to earn the same return on capital as a company in a competitive industry" (para. 260). "We consider that B.O.C.'s profits have been unjustifiably high for an almost complete monopoly facing a limited financial risk" (para. 261).

(b) "The prices charged by B.O.C. for oxygen and dissolved acetylene are too high" (para. 262).

(c) "In the case of a monopoly in the position of B.O.C. the prices which it charges should in our view operate fairly as between different customers and there should be no discrimination between customers in similar circumstances. B.O.C.'s present prices do not satisfy this condition, because they are not based upon the actual cost of supply to any individual customer or the average cost of supply to any class of customer" (para. 272).

(d) "The scales of charges should be based on relevant costs; and they should be made known to all consumers" (para. 275).

(e) "There does not seem to us to be any justification for any losses sustained on the sales of 'medical' oxygen being, in effect, carried by the industrial con-sumers" (para. 177).

(f) The Board of Trade or other competent authority should "satisfy itself by periodical reviews that effect was being given to our recommendations" (para. 280).

(g) "In view of the conditions of almost complete monopoly the opportunity should be taken to place every supplier of oxygen and dissolved acetylene under a duty to supply any bona fide consumer at a reasonable price provided that he has supplies available" (para. 282).

Further, I. C. Hill and Prof. Sir Arnold Plant argued, in their addendum, against a "national price" and observed:

(a) "Where costs vary widely either in production or transport, steps should be taken to ensure that such variations are reflected in the prices charged" (para. 297).

(b) "Although it may be sound policy for B.O.C. in its endeavour to maintain its monopoly to subsidize outlying areas at the expense of the more compact zones, such a distortion of price in relation to cost is against the public interest in so far as it restricts the possibility of specialized local competition in gases and adds to prices elsewhere" (para. 299).

(c) "An ex-works price plus a distribution charge based on zones of delivery would be in the national interest" (para. 299).

One may infer from these comments and recommendations that the B.O.C.'s monopoly practices have come in for greater discussion than the monopoly privileges of the nationalized industries.

[1] For a detailed discussion of the inter-Area shifts of benefit under the 1947 Act, see the author's book, *The Structure of the British Electricity Supply Industry*, pp. 135–55.

impossible. This part of our analysis could only be theoretical, as the Act has not yet been completely at work.

(a) To the extent that the Minister or the Electricity Council can influence the Boards' command of resources for expansion in such a way that some tend to be relatively more dependent on self-financing than others (who are helped by capital issues), there is bound to be a difference between the price levels—i.e., consumer burdens—in the two categories of Areas, at least in the short run.

(b) There are two possibilities, relevant to our discussion, under Section 14 (1). Firstly, "different tariffs may be fixed for different Area Boards." Theoretically, the Electricity Council may use this provision in order to justify different bulk tariffs, not based on grounds of costs of intake, but on grounds of rural electrification and the public interest. Though this depends on the way in which the Council[1] behaves in practice, the possibility cannot be ruled out, especially when the Board Chairmen by themselves fail to reach a unanimous decision. Secondly, the Generating Board, with an eye on self-financing, may succeed in fixing a bulk tariff that helps in building up a large generating reserve fund. Apparently all Area Boards benefit from the strength of this reserve. But their benefits are not uniform, unless the self-financing element of the bulk tariff is included in the fixed charge component of the two-part tariff. Where it is covered wholly or mainly by the running charge component, the Boards whose responsibility for maximum demand is relatively high gain as against the others.

(c) Under Section 19 (2) the Electricity Council can determine the annual contributions by the Boards to the central guarantee fund; and under Section 21 (1) it can require "any" of the Boards to contribute towards its expenses. The criteria to guide the apportioning of amounts among the different Boards are not specified in either case; and relatively unequal provisions cannot be ruled out.

### 3. *Clear rules*

From the above discussion it can be seen that the Boards' decisions touch on social policy upon which Parliament should pronounce, and that the provisions concerning ministerial intervention cannot be effective in keeping the Boards off policy matters. It would, therefore, be desirable to institute certain rules, in order to encourage objective performance by the Boards, and to provide for ministerial intervention only in respect of *residual* decisions having policy implications. Admittedly it is not possible to classify every issue as a

[1] The Electricity Council is composed of a Chairman, two Deputy Chairmen and all the Chairmen of the Electricity Boards.

purely commercial one or as a potential matter of policy. Almost every issue can be shown to contain some policy judgements; and many border cases exist—e.g., welfare expenditures, and privileges and facilities to be granted to different grades of employees. However, the underlying purpose of the rules is to provide definite criteria of commercial behaviour for the Boards and to exclude matters of policy from their routine administration.

There are two other advantages. Such rules provide us with the criteria of adjudging the performance of the Boards and would have an important role in ensuring their public accountability. If ever a consumer council, a committee of inquiry, a tribunal or an efficiency audit commission should investigate into or form a view on the working of the corporations, these rules would be the main basis from which to start; whereas in their absence, as at present, whatever criticism is made could be only a matter of opinion and, in any case, failure to observe statutory requirements cannot be attributed to the Boards. Essentially they contribute to the appropriateness of decisions as they are made and are, therefore, superior as an instrument of automatic vigilance on the Boards' decisions, unlike the investigations conducted at the end of a given period. The other merit of the rules is far-reaching indeed. To the extent that they offer clarity in decision making, they reduce the hesitancy of able men to join the Boards; and in an atmosphere fairly insulated from liability to criticism on grounds of social policy, it is possible not only to secure the best managerial talents but to obtain the best from them. Far from restricting the autonomy of the Board, these rules are intended to define it clearly and free it from subjective, arbitrary and political criticism, as far as possible. The following suggestions may be effected by regulations of the Minister, which have the merit of flexibility when compared with statutory amendments.

1. The first category of clear rules relates to the influences on Area Boards of the Electricity Council's or the Generating Board's actions.

(a) Section 14 (1), referring to the bulk tariff, should be clarified by a statement of the basis on which the bulk tariff is to be fixed, so that the "different tariffs" permitted for different Area Boards would be the reflection only of the cost conditions of intake of power. Either here, or at Section 20 relating to the Generating Board's reserve fund, the limits of annual and aggregate reserve accumulation as well as the general basis of its incorporation in the bulk tariff should be laid down, though not rigidly.

(b) Section 19 (2), under which the Boards should contribute to the central guarantee fund, should be revised so as to show the basis of the contributions. The fund is in the nature of a reserve to ensure interest payments, redemption of stock or repayment of Treasury guarantee payments. And it is laid down that "the moneys in the central guarantee fund shall not be applied for any other purposes". Though the reason for a central fund is legal in that the British Electricity Stock is the Council's responsibility, the respective financial liabilities of the Boards towards it could be easily traced to them individually; and no Board need contribute to the fund an amount out of proportion to its own obligations towards interest, stock redemption and guarantee repayments. Perhaps one reasonable basis would be to ask for contributions in proportion to the stock apportioned to the different Boards. This by itself would not remove the inequity of a Board contributing all the time without ever calling upon the fund to cover any default traceable to itself, unless individual accounts are maintained to show the contributions by and the utilizations for each Board and the necessary adjustments made from time to time with due regard to the basic rationale of the whole scheme. It may be hoped that Subsection (4), which permits periodical repayments from the fund to the Boards, if found necessary under "changed circumstances", performs this function in practice.

(c) Section 21 (1) under which the Boards contribute towards the Electricity Council's expenses, may likewise lay down the basis of spreading them over the Boards. If these are analogous to the costs of planning and external economies, they may be shared either in the ratio of bulk tariff payments or gross revenues or net revenues. There are arguments in favour of each of these methods; and the share of a Board varies with the method used. What is of importance is that any one method—perhaps the most acceptable one—must be adopted and applied consistently, to the knowledge of all the Boards.

2. The next category comprising the rules relating to the Area Board's own operations is a more important one.

(a) Section 13, which provides the financial fulcrum of the Board's performance, should be supplemented with appropriate rules of guidance covering the following aspects. (i) The financial targets should be less indeterminate and less discretionary and, subject to the requirements of reserve and self-financing, should be defined in relation to aggregate costs. (ii) Mention should be made of the largest possible output consistent with the over-all financial target so set; this target should be accompanied by a condition prohibiting a charge below marginal cost in any case.

(b) Section 14 (2) is too brief and general to be of great use in setting the complicated price relationships among different consumer-groups and regions; and consultation with the Consultative Council or with the Electricity Council would not help in this regard. It is necessary to lay down that the Boards shall promote, to a reasonable extent, such cost analysis as will indicate the costs to be borne by each major consumer group or region. Admittedly, what should be the size of the group or region, which is the deciding factor, is a controversial issue; yet the provision has the merit of promoting the right analysis in the right direction; and any interested consumer or assessor of Board performance would have the right tools at his disposal.[1] If the rule is supplemented with another requiring the Board, so far as is practicable, to relate the prices charged to the costs involved in any region or consumer group, the criteria of managerial behaviour will greatly improve at the top level as well as at the regional (sub-Area or enlarged district) level; and the canon of public accountability is at once enriched. What is more, transfers of benefit, which ought not to be caused by the Boards, would then be improbable or at any rate could be promoted only by conscious deliberation at ministerial or parliamentary level, followed by the necessary directions to the Board.

There are two other incidental benefits of a rule of this kind. Firstly, it would constitute a helpful limitation governing the uniform pricing tendency, and, while it allows of uniformity, as far as is consistent with the related-cost concept, it protects the Board from criticism on grounds of social policy. It would be easier for the public to judge whether the Board is keeping a "just balance"[2] between its clear commercial requirements and the general social expectations. The second advantage is in the realm of rural electrification. The Board would be obliged not to shift automatically the costs from one region to another.

An enthusiast for rural electrification would at once submit that the rule would defeat that idea; for regional pricing by related costs limits rural extensions more severely than over-all Area pricing by Area costs. The real point is that it brings the essential problems into the arena of public discussion. Should the burden of high-cost electrification be entirely borne by the region or consumer group concerned, by a whole Area as statutorily defined, by the whole industry comprising all the Boards, or by the public exchequer? The rule suggested has the merit of indicating the burdens involved, region by region; and it would be for Parliament to find the right answer and thereby enable the Boards to operate as objectively as possible. It

---

[1] Prof. P. Sargant Florence and H. Maddick comment on the ineffectiveness of the existing consumers' councils which lack the necessary data for putting up action. ("Consumers' Councils in the Nationalized Industries", *Political Quarterly*, July–September 1953.) The increased powers of the Councils under the 1957 Act do not, however, enable them to investigate into the fundamental issues relating to pricing.

[2] Select Committee on Nationalized Industries, para. 26 (1957).

would remove some of the anomalies mentioned in the earlier part of the discussion—e.g., varying objects of social policy resulting from the Boards' policies in the different Areas. Above all, it would help to realize that nationalization or the public corporation method offers no automatic solution of problems essentially social in character. Decisions on such questions must always be made by Parliament.

(c) Section 20 enables every Board to set up a reserve fund and to decide the amount and application of contributions to the fund; also it empowers the Minister to give directions in these questions. If the policy implications, as explained earlier, are to be kept out, it would be necessary to lay down the limits to the annual and aggregate contributions and the use of the fund for self-financing purposes. The importance of these rules cannot be too strongly emphasized in the context of resource allocation among public enterprises. The limits may be different, in absolute terms, in the different Areas, though, in relative terms, there should be a tendency towards consistency—e.g., in relation to gross earnings, needs of expansion and risks suffered.[1]

### 4. *Consequences of outside decisions*

Clear rules, as outlined above, go a long way in keeping the Board's decisions free from policy implications. In those cases where the Government wants the Board to implement a decision on grounds of policy, the value judgements relating to such decision are taken externally in so far as the Board is concerned; and it would be necessary to assess the consequences of such a decision in order that the results of the Board's own commercial behaviour remain separately assessable.

The point may be illustrated by reference to an existing provision —Section 28 (5) of the 1957 Act, under which "the terms and conditions" of supplying electricity to railway undertakers for haulage or traction may be determined by the appropriate Ministers, in case of non-agreement between the Board and the undertakers; and the only condition is that "these will not cause a financial loss to result to the Board from the provision of the supply". While this is a fair guarantee in itself, the ministerial intervention could easily distort the cost-price relationship in this case in comparison with that in the generality of the Board's operations. If the sale to railway undertakers is considered as a monopoly sale, the argument of protecting

---

[1] Section 22 (1), which empowers the Boards, subject to the Minister's directions, to apply their annual surpluses for such purposes as they determine, is covered by this suggestion.

the purchaser from a monopoly practice is understandable; but is the protection to come from the Ministers, who may tend to introduce considerations of inter-industry co-ordination and subsidization, or from an independent Tribunal—as in the case of bulk merchandise by the railways? After all, the transaction is not with a Department, but with an autonomous body, the British Transport Commission. If the ministerial determination is deemed necessary, it constitutes an example of a case which should be followed by an assessment of the consequences of external decision.

In conclusion, it may be noted that the object of these suggestions is to minimize the policy implications of pricing decisions by Boards rather than to provide a full list of pricing rules.

# CHAPTER IV

# THE CENTRAL ORGANIZATION FOR A NATIONALIZED INDUSTRY

THE question of a central organization for a nationalized industry arises mainly when a whole industry or a substantial part of it is in the public sector. It does not arise in the case of partial or full public ownership of certain undertakings in an industry (e.g., British Petroleum). If the enterprise is organized departmentally, it is probable that some kind of central organization will arise. For, (a) the cost-price relationship is less clearly defined in the case of a departmentally organized enterprise, is flexible and depends on the annual decisions of Parliament; in other words, those who are in direct charge of the enterprise are almost constantly in need of "external", i.e., central, decisions to guide them; (b) the canon of parliamentary accountability and the interest of uniform practice within the entire area of government operations places a heavy premium on the centralization of many a decision and decision-making process; and (c) since amenability to intimate control by Government is implicit in the choice of the departmental method, the formation of an all-embracing organization at the apex of the industry may well be a convenient step. Though certain elements of autonomy are permitted, as in the case of the British Post Office, the strength of the central organization as a managerial body remains unaffected.

It is when we turn to the public enterprise organized through the corporation method that the purpose of the central organization invites particular comment. Particularly is this so if the industry did not formerly have any central organization or had one but with quite different and perhaps simpler functions.

It is proposed, in this chapter (i) to suggest that the nationalized industry should be composed of optimal managerial units; (ii) to outline the purposes for which a central organization may be set up; (iii) to comment on the nature of the existing central organizations for the nationalized industries; and finally (iv) to examine certain relevant aspects of the regional boards.

## 1. *The arguments for and against a central organization*

To evolve a central organization primary consideration should be given to the objects with which nationalization was undertaken; some of them call for it more significantly than certain others. Four reasons may be mentioned to illustrate the point. (a) If the nationalization resulted from a desire to make the industry more economically organized than under private enterprise, the emphasis is on efficiency and, while the case for a central organization does not disappear, such organization need not be more elaborate than to ensure the maximum efficiency of the industry. (Of course full provision must be made for a progressive wage policy, labour welfare, joint consultation and consumer control, which ought really to form part of the desiderata of any industrial organization irrespective of the nature of ownership.) (b) Where nationalization was prompted by such specific objects as improving industrial relations or increasing capital expenditures, the case for a central organization may be limited to ensuring the attainment of those objects. (c) If the nationalization was intended to facilitate inter-consumer subsidizations, a central organization would be necessary for this purpose. (d) Lastly, where nationalization rested on the need for such planning as implies, not merely the removal of wastes through market imperfections, but a significant subordination of consumer freedom and the price mechanism to deliberate external decisions, it may be necessary to have a strong central organization that can influence the operations of the industry by external pressure. (Whether such planning is desirable, is outside the present discussion.)

While the case for a central organization, with powers of management or direction, is strong in the last two cases, it is debatable whether decisions on inter-consumer and inter-regional subsidies and planning which subordinates consumer choice should be left to the central organization. The nature of these decisions fits them for Parliamentary consideration.[1] If Parliament decides not to delegate these matters to the central organization, the function of the latter becomes limited to advising the Government and creating conditions for a smooth and efficient transmission of publicly approved policies to the managerial bodies within the industry.

The major difficulty in the present discussion is caused by lack of clarity about the objects of nationalization, not from the standpoint

---

[1] An example from private enterprise may be given to show that these decisions ought not to be left to a central monopoly unit. The British Oxygen Company, which has already been referred to, is in the nature of a monopoly central organization in the supply of oxygen and acetylene. The Monopolies and Restrictive Practices Commission made certain recommendations against its high profits and discriminatory pricing structures and suggested "an arrangement under which the Board of Trade or other competent authority was able to satisfy itself by periodical reviews that effect was being given to our recommendations". (Report on the Supply of Certain Industrial and Medical Gases, para. 281.)

of the Minister who introduced the bill or the majority of his party, but from that of the men entrusted with the management of the industry. For them the Act, the statutory instruments and the ministerial directions, governing their actions, are all that do and should matter. It seems that, by and large, the British nationalization Acts have emphasized the efficiency aspect of the industries concerned; and such expressions as "the public interest",[1] where they occur, do not suggest convincingly any particular shape of central organization. Earlier analysis has shown that the central organization should not take decisions based on non-commercial grounds.

If Parliament sanctions the attaining of certain objects other than efficiency and economy, by means of nationalization, these should be given statutory expression and followed by the creation of an effective central organization to achieve them. Where this is not done, the purpose of the central organization should mainly be to promote the efficiency of the industry.

There are five considerations to be kept in mind while devising the central organization. Firstly, the development of the most appropriate techniques of internal organization suited to the industry ought not to be prejudiced, e.g., in respect of delegation of decision-making powers or in promoting the conditions of efficiency at every level of management or operation. Secondly, there should be no automatic impact of conscious external decisions on the development of the industry, with scant regard for consumer preference. In fact it is a basic idea of the corporation method that the industry should be free from constant governmental influence. In other words, the decisions of the central organization ought not to be substituted, sometimes in the name of planning, for consumer preference as expressed through prices on such questions as what types and quantities of goods to produce. That is, the central organization ought not to help in the development of an uncontrolled monopoly. Thirdly, where the Government or Parliament wishes to influence the industry's operations in accordance with its policy decisions, there must be an organization which facilitates the process. Fourthly, conditions must be promoted for full public accountability in the sense of the most efficient performance of the industry, not only in the aggregate, but in each part. Lastly, certain welfare values, e.g., those concerning the workers and their place in the industry, or national values like the conservation of a resource, must be promoted more certainly than under private enterprise. In fact the case for promoting these is independent of the change in industrial ownership.

---

[1] E.g., Section 1 (c) of the Coal Nationalization Act, 1946, and Section 3 of the Iron and Steel Act, 1949.

89

## 2. *The concept of the central organization*

The term "central organization" refers to the organization at the apex of the industry. Where there can be only one optimal unit in the industry, under the prevailing conditions of costs and demand, the concept of a central organization is superfluous since it is co-extensive with the optimum unit itself. It is where the industry is or could be composed of more than one optimum managerial unit that the question of a central organization assumes importance.

The optimum managerial unit may now be defined. It is a unit which expands to the point of lowest cost without making any consumer or consumer-group worse off in the process of its expansion. Every consumer benefits from its growth in size, since it leads to additional economies in the fields of production, selling, financing and risk-taking. The test is whether a unit, which expands its activities beyond a given scale of output or beyond a group of consumers, can supply its products at a lower cost than previously. Up to the point where it ceases to do so, the expansion is justified and the resulting unit is an optimum unit. On the other hand, where such expansion causes disadvantage to one group of consumers because of another, e.g., rural electrification that raises urban tariffs, the resulting unit cannot be called an optimum unit in the sense visualized here. In fact such a unit would not develop if the forces of competition were powerful. (Under conditions of imperfect competition, which are widely prevalent today, inter-consumer shifts of benefit which go against the above tests are possible.)

It would be logical next to note the relationship between the optimum concept and the practice of price discrimination. Different prices for different consumer groups or different regions do not indicate necessarily that the undertaking has over-expanded so as to cause deliberate inter-consumer or inter-regional shifts of benefit. As long as each price is below the lowest possible cost at which, alternatively, an establishment suited to the scale in question could work, the large unit operating the different prices has its size justified on economic grounds. Wherever this test fails, the unit has exceeded the limits of optimum size.

There are two categories of price discriminations, where it is difficult to draw a conclusion. Firstly, the expansion of a unit may benefit one region or consumer-group without giving another a corresponding advantage or disadvantage. The complications in this case are: (i) that the expansion could place a new region or consumer-group at an advantage only because of some economy for which the original investment or capacity gave scope; and (ii) that no alternative supply on the scale required by the original region or consumer-group is possible at a lower cost. For these reasons such expansion may be of the desirable kind and so encouraged. The second situation is where the undertaking is free to choose between one region and another or between one consumer-group and another while offering a favourable price. In this condition considerations of social policy, to which the business unit could react differently, do arise. (To give an illustration, it is partly for this reason that railway freight classifications have been qualified by public regulation in many countries.) The desirability of expansion is not in question; but outside approval is desirable to determine the choice of beneficiaries.

Experience shows that there are four kinds of central organization:[1] (a) non-integrated, large regional boards like the Air Corporations of the U.K. and the Finance Corporations of India; (b) close integrations like the British Transport Commission (with a statutory London Transport Executive—and five others formerly—within it) and the former Central Electricity Authority (with fourteen statutory Area Boards within it); (c) loose federations like the Gas Council and the Electricity Council, with fairly independent regional boards; and (d) unitary command like the National Coal Board.

Whatever the nature of the central organization, it implies either a functional or a spatial unification of transactions, beyond the optimum limit; whereas a private unit generally expands within that limit either functionally or regionally. There is ordinarily a bias for organizing a nationalized industry on a regionally wide basis; and often the simplest of arbitrary decisions is taken, viz., to set up a nation-wide central organization. This then is one of the unsolved problems of public enterprise. What should be the size and functions of a central organization?

### 3. *Special factors in size evolution*

Let us turn to the widely held notion that nationalization implies the creation of large units—units larger in size than under private enterprise. If we accept as the desideratum the creation of optimum units, the basic question is: how does nationalization influence the process of optimal evolution? Three kinds of influences exist. Firstly, there are circumstances making for the expansion of unit sizes.

(a) Nationalization removes certain imperfections which may have stood in the way of optimum expansion in some cases, e.g., where the expansion of a small unit was prevented by a powerful rival or where the Local Authority undertakings in gas or electricity could not expand beyond the municipal limits.

---

[1] A fuller description is contained in section 5 of this chapter.

(b) Large units are favoured on grounds of economy in performing certain functions. Billing the customers and maintenance of installations may be cited as examples. The idea of providing enlarged districts with rough balance sheets of efficiency measurement was opposed by the Electricity Boards on the ground that it would duplicate specialist functions in each district and would, further, involve an uneconomic reduction in the scale at which certain services or processes could be performed.[1] Neither consequence need follow. For, all specialist services or functions whose economy depends on scale could be performed at the desirable level above the individual units and made available to them at a price. Inaccuracies may enter into decisions of identifying these separable functions; but in several cases the decision could be sufficiently objective. Where the functions centralized for specialized performance call for elaborate and arbitrary cost allocations and where the pricing of the services to the units becomes complicated, the individual units must be allowed to grow. For example, a fairly indivisible installation in the distribution of electricity may be treated as a unit, whereas installations whose costs are not common in the operating sense, though they may be in the over-all financial sense, need not be.

Secondly, there are influences in the direction of size limitation.

(a) Certain forces ordinarily leading to large sizes for the sake of low cost are weakened under nationalization. A private unit may find in largeness the advantages of low finance costs, few risks of demand diversion, wide spread of risks over business and strong bargaining power in the factor markets. These have a different significance for a nationalized industry. The finance costs are favourably influenced by Treasury guarantee, as long as it accompanies capital issues, and cease to be a relevant factor in size determination; whereas the other motives of spreading risks and greater bargaining power can be satisfied by inter-unit agreements which can be easily brought about. In fact it is possible for a nationalized body to focus more attention on the operating and managerial criteria in the formation of each unit than under private enterprise. The latter would take into account financial and strategic (or monopoly) advantages as well.

(b) Vertical disintegration of certain processes or services may, under private enterprise, be discouraged by the fact that it involves a cost as measured by the profit margins in the inter-unit transactions. It would materialize only when its economy exceeds this cost. Under nationalization there is no reason at all why this cost should be taken into account. By mutual agreement some or all units can transfer a certain process or function to a common specialist unit within the

---

[1] The Herbert Report, paras. 143, 295 and 297.

nationalized industry, e.g., research under the Electricity Council, and draw on it at cost, which by hypothesis is low. Each unit need not grow large for the sake of such cost economies in respect of the specialist functions; and none can perhaps grow so large as to achieve the largest possible economies.

Thirdly, there are considerations which are external to the inherent rationale of an industry's organization.

(a) The need for central marketing arrangements is mentioned in support of a large unit far beyond the optimum size. If the need is a social or political one, it can be implemented by transferring the marketing function to whatever level—national or regional—is felt desirable, or by imposing government control on the selling policies and prices, while keeping the industry free to develop the internal composition best suited to it according to its own economic criteria. Similar is the nature of the argument that "national" wage determination in the case of coal has an inevitable impact on the organization of the nationalized coal industry.[1]

(b) Large units help in averaging out regions and consumer groups with varying strengths of demand, thus making it possible for some of the regions and groups to obtain the product at relatively low prices. This is a "policy" consideration, whatever the exact nature of the cross-subsidization contemplated, and is therefore not strictly a matter within the essential objects of industrial organization. It may be seen, from the chapter on pricing and policy, that it is unjustifiable for the Boards automatically to effect price policies with tax effects; it may be added that the conditions for this to happen lie to no small extent in the statutory creation of "central organizations" in the sense of supra-optimum units.

### 4. *The purpose of a central organization*

The above analysis is intended as a logical step to show that, subject to the new circumstances introduced by nationalization, the nationalized industry should be organized primarily in terms of optimum units. A central organization may be set up in order to serve the following purposes.

(a) It may offer certain external economies more effectively than a trade association, e.g., (i) by carrying on research of basic interest to the entire industry, on which each unit cannot spend enough to make it expert and productive; (ii) by devising and conducting schemes for training the skills necessary for the industry; (iii) by taking charge of wage negotiations at a national level if such a

[1] For a discussion of this argument, see Clegg and Chester, *The Future of Nationalization.*

practice is suggested, if not insisted upon, by the attitudes of the workers; (iv) by undertaking common advertising in the interests of the industry as a whole; and (v) by conducting negotiations in connection with foreign contracts. These are all fields in which the central organization, while discharging its functions, does not infringe the managerial autonomy of the units within the industry. It would be preferable for these functions to be rendered on a permissive basis,[1] entitling but not compelling each unit to turn to the central services, though in the budgeting interests of the central organization some minimum contribution may have to be levied on each unit.

Further, the central organization can promote inter-unit knowledge of production and sales programmes, so as to avoid all preventable waste in their operations. In other words, it can remove certain causes of imperfection in the working of the industry. It is usual for the units of an industry to develop some mechanism of mutual information on their development programmes. This attempt would be reinforced by the creation of a central organization.

(b) It may create the conditions for the units to operate as appropriately controlled or controllable monopolies and satisfy the fundamental consumer interest of efficiency and objectivity in the managerial behaviour of the units. In order to fulfil this purpose, the central organization must work out a system for the organized provision of comparable data relating to the different units and of all those facts and figures necessary for assessing the commercial efficiency of every unit in relation to another. It need not pass judgements on a unit's working results but should present facts constructively to enable the public to draw their own conclusions. Specifically it may analyse the economic basis of the pricing policies of a unit with reference to (i) the statutory requirements, if any; (ii) the aggregate cost structure of the unit; and (iii) the different identifiable or separable consumer groups. Such an analysis is necessary in discovering whether and how the different units exercised monopoly power. Further, it may examine the "policy" implications —in the sense of social policy consequences—of certain pricing and other decisions of the units. These analyses may be made on its own initiative or at the instance of consumer bodies or the Minister. The need for the analyses is unquestionable; and it is desirable that the

---

[1] It would be interesting to refer to the Unilever's insurance unit which every part of the organization need not necessarily use. The Insurance Department at the centre can only suggest, recommend or persuade the individual units; but the latter are at liberty to obtain their insurances independently of their relative Insurance Department if they come to the conclusion that they can get better advice or service elsewhere. In practice, however, they find that they get the best advice and service from their own Insurance Department.

central organization, with its intimate and continuous knowledge of the industry, should produce them.

Fundamentally, we need to be clear on the permissible monopoly elements under nationalization. If a central organization (or a large monopoly unit) develops under private enterprise and is capable of introducing monopoly practices, there is a demand for bringing its activities under some kind of monopoly control. In cases where competition is not economical, some take the view that the inevitable monopoly organization must be transferred to the public sector. For example, two members of the Monopolies and Restrictive Practices Commission,[1] in their addendum to the Report on the Supply of Certain Industrial and Medical Gases, suggested for serious consideration the desirability of public ownership and management of the monopoly business of the British Oxygen Company. In their view adequate monopoly control in this case justified "a more far-reaching decision as to the future of this industry".

It is tempting to assume that nationalization is a remedial measure in the case of a monopoly industry. Unfortunately the basic problems of monopoly power are not solved by the measure *ipso facto*. Though the motive of high profit and private benefit ceases to exist, three aspects of the monopoly problem remain—viz., high costs through inefficiency, prices unrelated to costs, and output-and-investment policies unrelated to the price mechanism. These essentially require tackling even after nationalization.

The minimum requisite, therefore, is that the nationalized industry should not be so organized as to complicate the solution of the problems. It is in this field that enough success does not seem to have been achieved so far. A central organization which hampers the basic aims of monopoly control—these are basic, irrespective of the nature of the enterprise—has little to commend itself. For example, if it so operates that the constituent units can practise inter-consumer subsidization or varying cost-price relationships on their own and at random (that is, where these are not the result of parliamentary approval), it makes monopoly control more difficult than under private enterprise. It is even probable that in the course of time its actions will gain wrong prestige and political support, the basic economic considerations being lost sight of. And public ownership may then become "the most unpractical and the most cumbersome method of exercising public control that has ever been devised".[2] It is, therefore, best to evolve a central organization that helps in making monopoly practices improbable or easily challengeable, as

[1] A. Birch and W. L. Heywood.
[2] Duncan Sandys, Minister of Supply, *Hansard,* Vol. 508, col. 269.

long as our object is to remove monopoly evils rather than to see them practised by public enterprise.

(c) As long as the nationalized industry does not go to the market without a Treasury guarantee, the decisions on investment are deliberate and could be arbitrary, in regard to both the aggregate of outlays and their allocation among the different units, regions or purposes. If it is decided that the aggregate and the break-down should be left to ministerial, and political decision, there is no further room for discussion on grounds of economics or industrial organization. If, on the other hand, the decision should be guided by economic criteria, though eventually taken in the name of the Minister—and this seems to be the prevailing view in this country—there must be a proper machinery for the dispassionate marshalling of bids made by each managerial unit, in the context of the relative profitability, current and prospective, of the different units. In other words, a list of schemes in the order of economic justification should be drawn up, so that the final (ministerial) decision, which would be a substitute for the market mechanism, might rest on strictly economic criteria, as far as possible; and any decision taken for other reasons would at once be noticeable. The central organization may be entrusted with this preliminary work. Further, it may be asked to follow up the results of major schemes of investment in order to know how the results compare with the expectations. If, in the case of any unit, consistently wide gaps between the two are discovered, they reflect on the management's powers of expectation.

(d) In certain directions, the central organization could be of particular use to the Minister. Firstly, it would be available to him for prior and expert consultation on any of his functions with regard to the industry. Secondly, it could offer great assistance in the matter of ministerial appointment of members to top managerial posts within the industry—i.e., to the statutory Boards. The most appropriate system of making Board appointments is yet to be evolved; and it may well consist of a combination of the Minister, the central organization, an outside appointments or selection commission and a managerial training school. The school may give managerial training at the lower and intermediate levels; the commission may help in choosing persons from among them for higher managerial posts; the central organization may make recommendations to the Minister in the light of its knowledge of the industry and the persons concerned; and the Minister may announce the appointments to the Boards in the light of these preliminary processes. Thirdly, where the Minister makes a social or political decision which does not involve inter-consumer subsidizations, he may ask the central organization to work out the practical details so that the effects are spread over the entire industry. Where the policy has reference to the price structures and touches the relative interests of consumer groups or regions it should be so worked out in practice. While the Minister and his department ought not to work out the practical details of implementing the social or political decision, the central organization would outline the broad details, preserving a certain degree of the central character requisite in such a task. Fourthly, the Minister can ask the central organization to assess the consequences of external decisions on the commercial working of the units or the industry as a whole, whenever the information is deemed necessary.

Fifthly, the Minister would find it easier to take a decision which might be good for the industry though politically unpopular; for he could support himself on the ground of expert advice from the central organization for the industry. As this would not be a managerial body, the Minister could share with it the responsibility for decision making, though the decisions might eventually go in his own name. A non-managerial central organization may thus minimize political decision making at the ministerial level. Lastly, situations may arise when a unit proposes a price structure (or presents some other policy) which it claims to be in its commercial interest but which seems unpalatable to the Minister on other grounds. In his dilemma as to whether to give a direction or not, the question naturally arises as to whether the Board has an alternative policy to pursue, which would satisfy its commercial criteria and at the same time perhaps prove less unpalatable to the Minister. Today there is no way of discovering this, except by asking the Board to reconsider its decision. The central organization could be asked for advice in such a situation and, in view of its intimate knowledge, it could work out enough alternative data for further consultations between the unit and the Minister. It is possible that its ideas may be fresh and welcome to the unit itself. If, in spite of this process, a mutually satisfactory alternative cannot be found, then a direction may be necessary. This method makes the best decisions possible in a controversial situation and checks a unit in asking for a direction too frequently; for, if alternative decisions were frequently established as possible, the prestige of the unit and its managerial ability would be brought into question.

Briefly, the central organization, charged with the above functions, would be advisory to the Minister, would protect basic consumer interests, would promote the right allocation of resources to the industry and among its parts, and be capable of contributing to the solution of certain structural problems raised by the public corporation. It improves the present position where (i) the consumer has no means of challenging the pricing policies on grounds of inefficiency, undue discrimination or policy consequences not intended by Parlia-

97                                        D

ment, (ii) the Minister has no means of promoting the most appropriate long-term development of the industry, and (iii) there is a serious lack of such information on the Boards' policies as facilitates research by outside experts in the interests of the consumer and of the efficiency of the industry itself. Of course other methods of dealing with these difficulties could be devised—e.g., the extension of the jurisdiction of the Monopoly Commission or the inception of some similar Commission or Tribunal for the nationalized industries, the revision of consumer organizations, followed by the recruitment of competent staff, a departmental or some other organization for research into investment matters, and appropriate bodies to consider the policy implications of the Boards' pricing policies and to assess the consequences of external decisions on the Boards' commercial results. To some extent these arrangements would overlap and their operations might at times be inconsistent. A better experiment would be to revise the central organization of the nationalized industry, as suggested above, so that several objects could be achieved simultaneously.

The greatest merit of the proposal is the almost total termination of the managerial interest at the apex of a nationalized industry, followed by greater managerial autonomy at the lower regional levels as dictated by optimum considerations. The central organization would then have no interest in defending every aspect of the industry; nor need it behave as if it had responsibility for any particular aspect of the industry's operations. It is necessary for the success of the scheme suggested here that the central organization should not be conceived as an agency for passing judgements on the units within the industry, or as a formal channel in the hierarchy of decision intermediate between the Minister and the Boards, except in an advisory capacity. These two conditions, along with the guarantee of keeping the data confidential, would promote the required smoothness of relations between the units and the central organization.

## 5. Some practical aspects

None of the central organizations provided for the nationalized industries totally satisfies the concept given above. Further they are found to differ from industry to industry, in respect of the following separate responsibilities.

(a) *Formal responsibility*. All the central organizations bear formal responsibility for the capital stock; while the arrangements are not uniform as regards financial responsibility. For example, the former Central Electricity Authority had to present combined accounts and reports; while the Gas Council need not.

(b) *Regulating responsibility*. This concept is relevant in the case of non-monolithic organizations. The former Central Electricity Authority possessed several powers of regulating the whole industry —both generation and distribution; so did the former Iron and Steel Corporation; whereas the Gas Council's regulatory powers over the Gas Boards are nominal.

(c) *Planning responsibility*. Almost every central organization is entrusted with this responsibility; and three phases of it may be distinguished. (i) The Electricity Council, for example, has the duty "to promote and assist the maintenance and development by Electricity Boards in England and Wales of an efficient, co-ordinated and economical system of electricity supply". (Section 3 (4) (b), Electricity Act, 1957.) Similar is the Gas Council's duty—"to promote and assist the efficient exercise and performance by Area Boards of their functions" and "to secure the carrying out" (by the Boards) "of any general programme settled". (Section 2, The Gas Act, 1948.) The Iron and Steel Corporation had the general duty "to promote the efficient and economical supply of the products and activities specified".

It is relevant to note that the British Transport Commission's planning function partakes of inter-industry planning in that it has a duty "to provide, in such places and to such extent as may appear to the Commission to be expedient, other transport services"—i.e., road services (Section 25 (1), Transport Act, 1953). Its original duty, under the 1947 Act, was wider still—"to carry goods and passengers by rail, road and inland waterway within Great Britain". In other words, the British Transport Commission has always been in the nature of a central organization for different industries coming under the description of transport, with control varying in effectiveness between them.

(ii) Every central organization is entrusted with certain functions or powers in the interest of securing external economies directly or indirectly to the industry as a whole. Some examples are: to settle the programmes of research and secure their being carried out and to participate in joint consultations and national wage negotiations.

(iii) In many cases the central organizations are empowered, if not enjoined, to take into account non-commercial considerations. The Iron and Steel Corporation had "to further the public interest in all respects" and not to prejudice "such variations in the terms and conditions on which those products are supplied as may arise from ordinary commercial considerations or from the public interest".[1] The Coal Nationalization Act mentions the duty of

---

[1] Section 3 of the Iron and Steel Act, 1949.

"making supplies of coal available to further the public interest".[1]
The more the managerial functions are performed by the central
organization, the less desirable are powers enabling them to act for
non-commercial reasons. This is because, however necessary such
reasons may be from the national point of view, they involve inter-
industry choices or consumer–taxpayer preferences on which the
Government should decide.

(d) *Managerial responsibility*. This is paramount in the case of
monolithic organizations, of which the National Coal Board is the
best example, with its duty of "working and getting the coal in
Great Britain", apart from the planning responsibility of "securing
the efficient development of the coal-mining industry".[2] A similar
responsibility can, however, be established as resting, in the ultimate
analysis, upon central organizations like the former Central Electricity Authority, the former Iron and Steel Corporation and the British
Transport Commission, in that their powers involve managerial
decisions touching intimately on the entire range of the industry's
management. In any case, the aim would be that the combined
revenues of the industry do not fall short of the combined expenditure
of the industry. Perhaps it would be interesting, in view of the general
belief that the Iron and Steel Corporation preserved the managerial
autonomy of the companies, to cite the general duty of the Iron and
Steel Corporation—"to secure that those products are available in
such quantities, and of such types, qualities and sizes, and are available at such prices, as may seem to the Corporation best calculated
to satisfy the reasonable demands of the persons who use those
products for manufacturing purposes", "to avoid showing undue
preference to, and exercising unfair discrimination against, any
such persons or any class thereof in the supply and price of those
products, but without such variations in the terms and conditions on
which those products are supplied as may arise from ordinary commercial considerations or from the public interest."[3] Obviously these
functions go far beyond the general planning of the industry's development and encroach upon intricate managerial detail. The only
central organizations not charged with managerial responsibilities
are the Gas Council and the Electricity Council.

(e) *Advisory responsibility*. The Gas Council and the Electricity
Council are the only two central organizations which truly satisfy
this canon. The Gas Council is "to advise the Minister on questions
affecting the gas industry and matters relating thereto"; exactly

[1] Section 1 (1) (c) of the Coal Nationalization Act.
[2] Section 1 (1), Coal Nationalization Act, 1946.
[3] Section 3, Iron and Steel Act, 1949.

similar is the Electricity Council's duty.[1] Being non-managerial bodies, they are in a position to advise the Minister. In the case of the other central organizations like the National Coal Board and the British Transport Commission, the advice emanates from the party directly responsible for the operations; as such it may not be impartial.

At this stage reference may be made to the constitution of the central organizations. It may take one of three forms in its composition.

(i) The central organization may be completely independent of the personnel at lower levels—e.g., the British Transport Commission which does not include members of the London Transport Executive.

(ii) The central organization may be partly or significantly independent of the personnel at the lower levels—e.g., the former Central Electricity Authority which included four of the Area Chairmen (by rotation).

(iii) Where the central organization is mainly composed of the personnel at lower levels—e.g., the Gas or Electricity Council, which consists of all the Area Chairmen besides the Chairman and Deputy Chairmen. The second and the third constitutions are only suited to providing certain external economies for the industry as a whole. Matters of common interest may be discussed at meetings where all the units are represented. Broad conclusions should then be reached, in the light of which each unit would proceed autonomously to work out its own policies and programmes. In other words, they could operate as the replica of a trade association in certain aspects of their business. For all the other functions of the central organization outlined above, a constitution exclusive of the personnel at lower levels is necessary. This would not be an undesirable or dangerous development, since the central organization would neither control the units nor initiate plans or decisions for them. The new conception essentially involves a change in the status of the central organization which would be converted into an expert agency for certain public purposes *vis-à-vis* the nationalized industry. This would provide a means of compensating for the loss of market tests as a measure of the success of its operations. The chairmen of the units might be formed into an Advisory Council to deal with the arrangements for external economies and centralized services.

In order to discharge its functions successfully, the central organization should have five wings under it respectively concerned with (i) consumer interest, in the broad sense of making the units function as controlled monopolies, (ii) investment questions, (iii) policy

---

[1] Section 1 (1) of the Gas Act and section 3 (4) of the Electricity Act, 1957.

matters, i.e., policy consequences of Boards' decisions and the results of external decisions upon Board's finances, (iv) common purposes to promote external economies for the units, and (v) general questions of comparison concerning the whole field of public enterprise and corporation autonomy. The last section has some of the characteristics of the "common efficiency unit" suggested by Herbert Morrison[1] and may contribute partially to the solution of certain constitutional questions of ministerial interference with the corporations.[2]

The consumer bodies cannot, under present conditions, function effectively in respect of broad questions concerning, for example, the level of prices, price discriminations, cross-subsidizations and alternative programmes of development. One of the remedies suggested by P. Sargant Florence and H. Maddick contains an important principle. This is that machinery should be provided to enable the consumers to assess the efficiency of the Boards and the merits of their policies.[3] If the central organization is evolved on the suggested lines, it would only be necessary to form a small Executive of the consumer bodies jointly to investigate broad points of policy. The fact that the central organization should have its own initiative in such investigations considerably improves the position. This arrangement also has the advantage of entrusting fact-finding and analysis to an agency intimately connected with, but not managing, the industry instead of to an outside organization formed as an investigating body.[4]

It is relatively unimportant whether, under the new scheme, the formal financial responsibility for the capital stock would continue to rest with the central organization. As it is, in the case of electricity, it does rest *de jure* with the Electricity Council, though it is clear from the Act that *de facto* it rests with the individual Boards. The object of the central guarantee fund is only to provide against a demand on the Treasury guarantee in the event of the temporary inability of a Board to contribute in full towards its share of interest charges. It should be recognized that formal financial responsibility

---

[1] Herbert Morrison's suggestion is a much broader one. "It (the common efficiency unit) should be a common product of the Boards collectively, and could be used as industrial consultants." (Q. 384, Report from the Select Committee on Nationalized Industries, 1953.)

[2] Lord Reith suggested in this respect the setting up of a "minister for nationalized industries" as "one possible way" (*ibid.*, Q. 647–9).

[3] Prof. P. Sargant Florence and H. Maddick, "Consumers' Councils in the Nationalized Industries", *Political Quarterly*, July–September 1953.

[4] This is not a suggestion that circumstances do not arise, in which an impartial outside committee of inquiry is desirable.

at the national level does not *ipso facto* require any managerial responsibility at the same level.

At this stage a brief digression may be introduced concerning the Iron and Steel Board set up under the Iron and Steel Act, 1953. It is not a central organization for the industry in the sense in which the term is employed in this chapter. It is established "for the supervision of the iron and steel industry", which is inherently a governmental function. The Minister of Supply stated that "there are three fields in which some measure of public supervision is necessary: prices, development and raw materials";[1] and such supervision, if necessary, is necessary irrespective of whether the enterprise is in private or public hands. In being required to "have regard to any considerations relating to employment in Great Britain or otherwise relating to the national interest to which the Minister may have asked them to have regard",[2] the Board is in a different position from most of the central organizations for the nationalized industries, which are in the nature of managerial bodies.

The Board is intended as a compromise between rigid central planning on the one side, and a totally competitive framework of industrial organization on the other.[3] Some of the items specifically brought under its supervisory purview are: the productive capacity of the iron and steel producers, the procuring and distribution of raw materials and fuel; the prices; the promotion of research and training; the safety, health and welfare of the employees; and joint consultation. Further, the Board has to "act as agent" for the Minister in the exercise of his functions[4] and "give advice and information" to him in respect of the European Coal and Steel Community matters.[5]

The Act has an emphasis against the Board touching on internal detail of the iron and steel units. For example, Section 15 entitles the Board to ask the producers only for information "not relating directly to the costs of production"; and in explanation of Section 6 (1) which makes expansion of any unit conditional on the Board's permission, the Minister stated, while introducing the Bill, that only "big expansion schemes in the heavy end of the industry" were contemplated.[6]

It is difficult to say how far the Board was devised as a political

---

[1] Duncan Sandys, *Hansard*, Vol. 508, col. 268.

[2] Section 5 (2), Iron and Steel Act, 1953.

[3] Section 3 (1) lays down: "It shall be the duty of the Board to exercise a general supervision over the iron and steel industry . . . with a view to promoting the efficient, economic and adequate supply under competitive conditions of iron and steel products."

[4] Section 3 (2), *ibid.*

[5] Section 4 (2), *ibid.*

[6] *Hansard*, Vol. 508, col. 275.

compromise between the continuance of iron and steel as a nationalized industry and its total denationalization. It is equally difficult to say whether the functions of the Board may not be altered by the future Governments. At the moment one may view the Board as a public body entrusted with a governmental function which, in any case, has to be carried out. The unique point is that, unlike with most other private enterprises, there is a statutory supervisory-cum-advisory body functioning all the time. It offers the advantage of expert, fairly independent, supervision of the industry, as compared with direct supervision by a government department; and it preserves the system of autonomous managerial units within the industry.

## 6. *The regional boards*

Let us briefly discuss one aspect of the rationale of the regional boards—e.g., the statutory Electricity or Gas Boards. Wherever a regional board is in the nature of an optimum managerial unit, as defined in Section 2, its size is economic and, therefore, quite justified. If, on the other hand, it is composed of more than one optimum unit or could be subdivided into more than one optimum unit, there is a supra-optimal element in the regional board. In so far as the individual units are concerned, the regional board has some of the characteristics that the central organization itself has in relation to the regional boards. If the industry is organized in terms of optimum units, there is no reason why there should be a regional organization intermediate between the optimum units and the central organization, except for the provision of common services and the promotion of certain other external economies for the units coming within an area. With this limited purpose in view, the size of the regional organization should really depend on the most economic scale for the actual function or service in question. In order to simplify organization a single regional organization covering some units might be set up and entrusted with certain functions, though the optimum scales are not co-extensive for all the functions. Wherever the interests of specialization and economy indicate further centralization, the functions may be raised to the level of the central organization itself.

There is another argument in support of a regional organization. Despite meticulous cost imputations, there may still remain certain indivisibilities in the factors of production whose incidence on each unit is best worked out by a system of cost allocation. And accurate pricing of the services in question might be difficult. When we approach a situation of this nature, e.g., in the case of overlapping distribution installations in the electricity industry, an equally justified course would be to establish a regional organization which, subject alone to such residual cost allocations, would let every unit operate with substantial managerial autonomy.

Let us turn to two non-economic arguments in favour of the regional organization. Firstly, nationalization automatically raises the question of public accountability. In this respect it might be easier for the public or Parliament to understand the issues involved, assess the proper working of the industry and feel satisfied with the efficiency of the Boards when there are a few units with independent results than when there are many such units. There is no principle involved here, except that of convenience of numbers; e.g., results of fourteen boards are more convenient to study than those of forty units. In fact if the argument is extended, a single unit is even more convenient, though many seem to prefer a few regional boards as a practical compromise between the convenience of public assessment and the undesirability of a monolithic nation-wide monopoly. With the new kind of central organization envisaged here, a greater compromise is possible with the proposed larger number of independent units; for the central organization itself is helpful as a means of achieving public and parliamentary understanding of the multi-unit industry.

Secondly, there is support for a regional organization in order to facilitate regional cross-subsidizations, which would be made possible by the managerial and financial unification of operations in heterogeneous and regionally different markets. A nation-wide unit would achieve it more excellently—e.g., the National Coal Board and the British Transport Commission. Here again there is a compromise, not on grounds of economics so much as by reason of other and sometimes arbitrary considerations, between nation-wide cross-subsidizations (accompanied, further, by the managerial difficulties of a super-sized business unit under nationalization) and the total absence of any cross-subsidization. To average out good and bad markets together might be a vague object of nationalization, though the limits to such an approach are unclear. Whether there should be cross-subsidization among optimum units, and, if so, of what pattern, is a matter on which Parliament, not the regional organizations, should decide. The regional organization should, however, show the relative financial efficiencies of the different units under it, so that Parliament has clear data on the extent and structure of inter-regional shifts in benefit, which are more analogous to the effects of taxation than of pricing. The evolution of optimum units essentially has, as an ideal, the connotation of the most efficient management and the most economic costs of performance, irrespective of whether the financial ends of the different units are unequally set and of whether some are expected to subsidize the others.

It is difficult to make generalizations on the optimal nature or otherwise of the several regional boards operating within the nationalized industry, without carefully analysed factual evidence in each case. In order to translate the above ideas into practice, it is necessary to demarcate the optimum units under each regional board (in the industries where such a board exists) and work out a fairly distinct financial statement for each unit, subject to the necessary residual cost allocations. There are two requisites in this connection, viz., that the statute should require each regional board to organize itself in terms of optimum, separately assessable units and that the demarcation of these units, being a conscious one, should be done with adequate care and objectivity; and difficulties in border-line cases ought not to be adduced as an argument against the whole scheme.

Two further points may be noted. Once the regional board is subdivided into optimal managerial units, it need not discharge managerial functions to the same degree as at present. It only serves certain over-all purposes mentioned above. Secondly, for these changes to take place it is not necessary to confer statutory autonomy on every optimum unit. Legally a few optimum units may work within a regional board, though in point of actual working they retain the necessary characteristics of managerial autonomy.

## 7. Conclusion

The purpose of the discussion has been to show that: (i) the fundamental interest of the community *vis-à-vis* a nationalized industry, in the field of organization, lies in the evolution of optimum units that ensure the lowest cost of performance; (ii) the test of optimum expansion is that no region or consumer-group is worse off on account of the expansion; (iii) price discriminations beyond those justified in the process of optimum expansion amount to cross-subsidizations; (iv) the rationale of an organization beyond the optimum level needs a thorough analysis and the objects of central organization should be kept to a minimum; (v) arrangements on these lines would not be inconsistent with the implementation of the broader social or economic policies of which Parliament approves; and (vi) the central organization, under the new concept, would fill certain institutional gaps in the evolution of nationalization and the public corporation, while automatically improving the managerial conditions under which the units of the nationalized industry operate.

# DISCRIMINATION AND CROSS-SUBSIDIZATION

IT is desirable to use precisely the terms "discrimination" and "cross-subsidization",[1] which are often found in discussions on nationalized industries. This note aims to show the difference between the two concepts in the field of pricing. In connection with the working of the nationalized industries, it is important to distinguish these terms because it is suggested that discrimination is what the managers of nationalized industries may operate on their own responsibility, whereas cross-subsidization falls outside their legitimate managerial area.

The common symptoms of both discrimination and cross-subsidization are that different prices are charged to consumers for similar products involving the same delivered costs, that equal prices are charged to consumers for products involving different delivered costs, or that unequal prices, which are out of proportion to the cost differentials, are charged. Here cost refers to the average cost; and a single product and the property of non-transferability are assumed.

## 1. *Discrimination*

The term discrimination connotes unequal prices. But there is an important condition under competition. No price can be higher than the cost at which alternative supply is possible in the market concerned. (The size of the capacity, from which the alternative supply emanates, would be qualified, firstly, by the physical indivisibility of the installations necessary to serve the market in question and, secondly, by the convenience of catering for other markets in conjunction with the market in question.) The real point is, not that the price in market A is higher than the price in market B—under identical cost conditions—but that the price in A is lower than the price at which an alternative supply is possible in market A.

Under conditions of competition, a firm expands, treating several markets compositely and at different prices, only so long as no individual price is so high as to attract a fresh entrant into the

---

[1] The term cross-subsidization has been used in economic literature to denote the subsidization of one consumer by another, though strictly the term should imply subsidization of one consumer by another in return for another subsidization in the reverse direction—on the analogy of the term "cross-haul".

market concerned. In other words, the expansion is such as leads to cost diminution to be followed by a price reduction or, anyway, no price increase, to the existing consumer. In an extreme case he may be neutral to a new customer being served at a price equal to the marginal cost involved, provided that no addition to the fixed costs is involved. It is true that questions touching on income distribution arise in this case; for should the new consumer be given the benefit of the lower price? It is true that the lower price would not have been possible but for the existing consumer. Nevertheless, the latter is no worse off when the new consumer is served.

The test of alternative cost of supplying a market fails under conditions of monopoly, characteristic of many nationalized industries. And the familiar justification that a new consumer making some contribution to the non-marginal costs is welcome to the existing consumer is inconclusive. Though it might be valid in the case of a given plant, the very concept of a given plant is question-begging under the organization of a nationalized industry. It is necessary to ask whether the given plant is of the right size, considering the interests of each market and whether, if a smaller capacity were set up, that would not ensure lower costs and, therefore, lower prices in that market. It is, therefore, necessary to conduct cost analyses with a view to establishing whether a given capacity—say a regional board —exceeds the limits of an optimum unit and whether smaller units could be identified and separated out with the advantage of lower costs of supply in the markets concerned. Probably the cost analyses are not precise, since at times computations on non-existing bases may be involved. Yet they are sufficient to give broad conclusions.

Discrimination is justified within the optimum size of a unit. That ensures the economical organization of the industry in the sense that each unit of business expands up to the limits of economy in cost or, broadly, in the use of resources. At the same time the test of no price being higher than that possible with a smaller capacity ensures that no consumer is at a disadvantage in the process of expansion. Such price discrimination may be treated as coming within the purview of the managers. In a few cases like the one cited earlier, income effects are possible, on which the managers ought not to be the arbiters. The Government may deal with such cases, under the method of directions or statutory instruments.

Discrimination, under which every price exceeds related total cost, is one form of the profit-maximizing process and is possible under conditions of monopoly. It could also be a means of earning for the general exchequer revenues, if the financial arrangement between the Government and the nationalized industry permits of a transfer of the profits to the Government. It falls outside the scope of the present discussion; and its justification depends on the view taken on the question of monopoly profits and of making the nationalized industries a means of indirect taxation.

## 2. *Cross-subsidization*

The essential difference between cross-subsidization and discrimination is that, while one market gains by the test of either full imputed cost or the cost of alternative supply, another loses in the case of cross-subsidization but not in the case of discrimination.

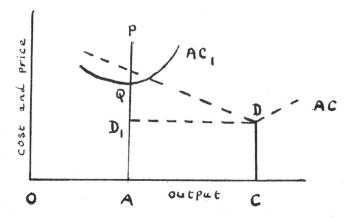

Assume that AC is the average cost curve for a firm operating at OC, at cost CD per unit, that AP is the price charged in one market A, and that $AC_1$ is the alternative possible cost curve for the scale of demand OA. Any price between $AD_1$ and AQ, in the market OA, would be in the nature of justifiable discrimination, *vis-à-vis* prices in the market AC lower than the average costs; whereas any price above AQ has in it the element of cross-subsidization.

Such cross-subsidization is possible only with a monopoly organization; while justifiable discrimination is not impossible with an optimum unit in a competitive field. Even if the monopoly were no larger than an optimum unit, as represented by AC in this case, let us assume, pricing above AQ in market A does amount to cross-subsidization, though it would be hidden; and where the monopoly organization is supra-optimal in size, the cross-subsidization is obvious.

It follows that one of the considerations in determining whether a given capacity is optimal or supra-optimal in size is to see whether the different parts of the capacity are so bound together technologically, or in any other way, that the costs are inter-dependent in the sense of every part gaining in its cost conditions from its integration with the other parts within a single managerial unit. If any part is discovered as capable of being isolated as a production-cum-selling unit, without its cost position being affected unfavourably, the given capacity, of which it is a part, is in the nature of supra-optimal capacity; and discrimination against the markets in that separable part could really be in the nature of cross-subsidization.

This is perhaps the only way in which the cases of discrimination could be distinguished from those of cross-subsidization on the railways. Low rates on certain sections might be an instance of discrimination and therefore permitted, if those sections formed an integral part, in the above cost sense, with some other sections on which rates are higher. Whereas, low rates on certain sections would be an instance of cross-subsidization if this test failed, i.e., if the sections on which higher rates are charged could be worked as separate units with cost advantage to themselves.

The price AP is possible only because no alternative supply is possible. The question of whether the price AP, at which there exists demand, should not be charged, is excluded from the present discussion, as it is not very relevant to the point under analysis, except for one aspect. (It has been assumed that the industry tries to cover its costs, including those of replacements and reserves.)

Assume that the industry tries to make a surplus over and above its recoverable costs, including interest; and that this policy might lead to a price of AP in the market A, as against prices lower than costs in the market AC. Whether this is cross-subsidization of market AC by the consumers in market A depends on the purpose of the surplus. The surplus may be earned for two reasons—either for the industry's own purposes, like self-financing, or for transfer to the general exchequer. In the former there is cross-subsidization; while in the latter case it is not cross-subsidization that prevails but a system of unequal prices as a means of indirect taxation. Whether the managers should decide on the structure of inequalities in prices, which are tantamount to a tax incidence, is an open question. But the point is clear that consumers paying the high prices do not pay for the sake of other consumers; they pay for the relief of the taxpayer.

Under the British Nationalization Acts, the surpluses resulting from the industry's operations remain with the industry itself. Hence profits resulting from unjustifiable discrimination—unjustifiable in the light of the argument presented in this discussion—imply cross-subsidization of some consumers by others.

Four questions arise in this connection: (i) Are the consumers of *this* product in market A necessarily rich enough to be taxed? (ii) Should they be taxed for the benefit of some other market served by the monopoly? (iii) Why should they be chosen to contribute, as against the taxpayers in the region helped or the general taxpayers as a whole? (iv) Has Parliament debated the issue or approved the implications of the pricing policy?

These questions need public discussion and answer by Parliament; and it would be desirable to require the nationalized industries to organize themselves into optimum units so that price differentials generally tend to lie within the area of discrimination, as against cross-subsidization. Even if a large formal organization is set up for reasons of convenience, it should work *de facto* on the principle of optimal sub-units; and policies involving cross-subsidization should be publicly decided.

# CHAPTER V

# THE PUBLIC ACCOUNTABILITY OF A NATIONALIZED INDUSTRY

THE question of public accountability of a nationalized industry assumes significance when it is not managed by a government department. A departmentally organized enterprise is directly under the control of the Minister and the elected representatives of the people. Once the decision has been made that the compromise with the efficiency canon implicit in the departmental form is suited to the enterprise in question, few further problems arise; and the Minister is "accountable to Parliament for anything he or his Department does or for anything he has powers to do, whether he does it or not". "But the principle of parliamentary accountability does not hold the Minister responsible for things which Parliament has already decided he is not responsible for."[1] Most of the corporation's activities belong to this category; hence the specific problem of ensuring its accountability.

It is proposed, therefore, to devote the discussion mainly to the public accountability of the public corporation and in the end touch on the question as applied to another form of non-departmental organization—namely, the joint stock company.

The plentiful literature on the public accountability of the corporation gives the impression that the term is often treated as synonymous with the amenability of the corporation to some kind of public control, in view of its peculiar constitutional freedom from direct shareholder control. Such freedom is not associated with private enterprise or a departmental business. Parliament has taken the initiative in converting the concept into one of parliamentary control. Since this, however, might seem to be incompatible with the very conception of the corporation as a "self-denying ordinance"[2] on Parliament's part, some kind of a distinction between "major policy" and "management" is sought to be upheld; and the former envisaged as a fit matter for public or parliamentary control.[3]

[1] Herbert Morrison, *Government and Parliament*, p. 256.

[2] Lord Reith Q. 593, Report from the Select Committee on Nationalized Industries, 1953.

[3] Lord Reith observed that the public corporation system "should give public control over major policy but no public interference in management". (Q. 604, *ibid.*) To the question "would it then be your opinion that the committee should, as far as possible, confine itself to questions of policy and should confine its

Further, most of the thought on the subject has been directed towards the inception of some body with a degree of investigatory power. Herbert Morrison himself suggested, as alternatives to the Select Committee, a B.B.C.-type of Inquiry[1] and a common efficiency unit, which, he agreed, would together meet "any deficiency in public accountability or Parliamentary accountability at the present time".[2] His common efficiency unit is not, however, identical with an investigatory body, as we shall see later.

On the whole relatively small emphasis has been placed on the more important requisite, viz., the establishment of criteria or canons by which the corporations are expected to be accountable. In short, the question has been treated, by and large, in terms of to which body the corporation shall be accountable rather than by what criteria it shall be held accountable. The latter course has the merit of clarifying what is expected of the managers of the corporations— beyond the steam-roller financial provision of "not less than . . .";[3] and would substitute objective judgements on set standards for the possibility of subjective assessments by investigatory agencies. This is not a plea against the setting up of an agency to express opinions on the public accountability of a corporation; on the other hand, the suggestion is that even such a body must be provided with the criteria on which it may base its judgements. In an extreme case, investigatory bodies, in the absence of set criteria of accountability, could only point out past mistakes without offering the managers valid criteria to follow in a subsequent period; and except for the inferences from the criticized past actions, no guiding principles would be available for future managerial behaviour.

An incidental offshoot of Parliament's approach to this question has been the development of the idea that "informing Parliament" is a basic element of the concept of public accountability. In fact the Select Committees set up in 1951 and 1952 were "to consider the present methods by which the House of Commons is informed of the affairs of the Nationalized Industries and to report what changes . . . may be desirable in these methods."[4] The integral relationship between the idea of informing Parliament and the concept of public accountability seems to have gained subsequently

conclusions to such inferences as can be drawn from the accounts rather than meddle in questions of managerial efficiency," Hugh Molson said, "that is so." (Q. 329, *ibid.*)

[1] An inquiry once in seven years, as in the case of the B.B.C.

[2] Q. 476, Report from the Select Committee on Nationalized Industries, 1953.

[3] Section 13 of the Electricity Act, 1957.

[4] Report, 1953 (*op. cit.*), p. ii. The Committee set up in 1955 was "to obtain further information" (over and above what the Reports contained) subject to certain qualifications.

from the focus laid by that Committee on the establishment of a Select Committee for ensuring greater public accountability. If evidence in support of this interpretation were required, none is better than Lord Hurcomb's opinion that "I think it (the Committee) would make accountability a two-way process. Parliament would feel it had got some knowledge which it does not now get."[1]

## 1. *The concept of public accountability*

The concept of public accountability is a wide one. Though its origin may be traced to the completion of separation between ownership and management, it has an extensive connotation, derived essentially from the problems raised by the newly evolving institution of public enterprise through the medium of the corporation. Briefly, public accountability may be defined as a framework of assurance: (a) that the commercial performance of the corporation is efficient, both in the short run and in the long run; (b) that the Board's decisions shall not contain implications of social policy[2] but shall be based on commercial criteria in the main; (c) that any parliamentarily approved or ministerially directed decisions are implemented in practice; and (d) that the Minister, as distinct from the Board, shall be accountable for his own influence on the Board's working. The concept would be truncated if any of these elements are not properly provided for; and too much or exclusive attention to any one of these desiderata at the expense of the rest produces unhealthy results in the context of ensuring public accountability.

(a) The commercial efficiency of the industry, expected of the Board, is in itself a multi-phased concept, though it is sometimes classed as a single idea and its yardsticks are subjects of debate. It divides itself into three aspects: (1) the consumer interest, viz., that production and selling are most economic and pricing policies most rational, that optimum units of business are evolved and that there is no wrong exercise of monopoly power leading to "cross-subsidizations"[3] or any other evils; specific indices of technical efficiency or productivity are some of the means of assessing how far this interest is satisfied;[4] (ii) the taxpayer's interest that the activities of the corporation shall not result in a loss, for that would at least immediately fall on the

---

[1] Report, 1953 (*op. cit.*), Q. 543.

[2] For a discussion of the "policy" implications of the Board's decisions see Chapter III.

[3] For a definition and discussion of "cross-subsidization", see the Appendix on "Discrimination and Subsidization".

[4] For a discussion of the indices of efficiency of nationalized industries see P. Sargant Florence and Gilbert Walker, "Efficiency under Nationalization and its Measurement", *Problems of Nationalized Industry*, edited by W. A. Robson.

114

public exchequer (as exemplified by the British Transport Commission's financial position);[1] and (iii) the over-all national interest that there shall be no misallocation of resources among the public enterprises. It is at once clear from this analysis that some of the canons cannot be satisfied by the corporation exclusively. Allocation of resources, for example, is, by current practice as well as statute, a matter for which the responsibility for decision is mainly ministerial. The experience of the London Transport Executive suggests that even the losses are not always the product of exclusively *de facto* Board decisions. Further, the satisfaction of the consumers' interest of efficient operation is itself under the influence of external policies, e.g., in the field of investment.

Attention should be paid to these three interests under the new conditions where there is substantial interference with the normal economic forces characteristic of a private enterprise.

(b) It is not clear that every nationalization is inspired by a positive desire to employ the pricing and other policies of the enterprise in such a way as to achieve the purposes of the government budget. In the case of nationalization organized as a corporation it is less clear that the Board should act like a taxing agency or judge between alternative regions or groups on social or political grounds, introducing consciously or otherwise value judgements in decision making. It is, therefore, necessary for the public and Parliament constantly to be assured that the corporation does not, without their knowledge and approval, indulge in broader actions than are justified on strict commercial grounds. This is because the basic reason for choosing the corporation form is that, within the broad limits set by Parliament, it shall act as an expert commercial organization, relieved of the weight of political and social pressures. To illustrate corporation decisions touching broader social issues the London Transport Executive's attitude to unprofitable services may be cited.[2]

[1] For details, see Proposals for the Railways, British Transport Commission, October 1956, Cmd. 9880.

[2] The Executive's view is: "A third choice theoretically open to the Executive of cutting out the most unprofitable services must be discarded, because such a policy could only result in certain districts or groups of passengers being deprived of public transport altogether while others were untouched. It would cause intense hardship to certain sections of the community. Such a course would be quite unacceptable and would be inconsistent with the Executive's obligation to provide an adequate service over their whole area. . . . It is also important to be clear that the fact that a particular service is unremunerative is no evidence whatever that it is less necessary from the standpoint of public need than the generality of services that pay. On the contrary, there are many services which are unremunerative in themselves yet would be generally recognized as essential to the community's economic health and social life . . . the Executive's decisions in regard to the provision of such (i.e., uneconomic) services are governed by their

(c) However, where Parliament or the Minister decides on a policy other than that dictated by the commercial considerations which the Board ought mainly to take into account, the policy must be implemented by the Board. It would now be necessary for Parliament to be assured that it has been put into practice and to know whether the intended results have been obtained.

(d) It is easy to deduce from certain provisions of the Acts[1] and from experience that many decisions of the corporation are influenced by the Minister, statutorily or informally,[2] though the method of direction has on the whole not been widely used. There seem to be four situations involving ministerial influence: (i) where the Act makes a condition that Board actions are subject to consultation with and approval of the Minister, as in the case of settling research or investment programmes; (ii) where the Minister's "responsibility" is "engaged";[3] (iii) where the Minister issues a direction; and (iv) where the Minister exerts informal influence or pressure. It is in the first and the third cases that the Minister's responsibility, as distinct from the Board's, is fairly clear; while in the other two cases it is difficult to distinguish the Board's autonomous behaviour from ministerial influence. Obviously the Board has to be held responsible for its autonomous actions only; and opinions on its efficiency or accountability, if based on such actions only, are justified, and useful. In a situation where its autonomous commercial behaviour and external influence cannot be distinguished—and the consequences of the latter cannot be broadly estimated—conclusive judgements on the Board's public accountability are not possible.

## 2. *Ensuring public accountability*

It is now clear that the connotation of public accountability is so

---

judgement of the public need." The Chambers Committee observed," in effect, the British Transport Commission and the London Transport Executive take the view that under the Acts they are the arbiters of the public need for transport." (Report of the Committee of Inquiry into London Transport, 1955, p. 17.)

[1] For example, sections providing for Ministerial consultation or approval.

[2] Referring to the "Gentleman's Agreement" on coal prices, the Select Committee on Nationalized Industries observed, in April 1958, that they "do not like its informality. Although it binds the Board, and vitally affects the way they work, it is based on no more than a letter from the Minister" (para. 89).

[3] In fact 58 specific responsibilities of the Minister and 3 powers of direction were listed out with reference to the British Transport Commission, 21 and 4 in the case of the Air Corporations, 56 and 6 in the case of coal, gas and electricity, and 41 and 6 in the case of electricity in Scotland. (Select Committee Report, 1955.)

broad and composed of such diverse issues that exclusive insistence on certain elements of it would fall short of the real expectations of the community in the working of the corporation. To say that efficiency is what is required of the corporation amounts to an over-simplification, for it has little meaning unless all the four criteria mentioned above are kept in view and followed up.

In view of the broad implications of the concept of public account-ability, no single body or method may help in fulfilling it. The in-adequacy of the Parliamentary Select Committee may now be appre-ciated. It is doubtful whether Parliament or the Select Committee is necessarily competent[1] to investigate, or express an opinion on, the commercial efficiency of the corporation;[2] it has responsibility, how-ever, for securing the remaining three objectives. Even here, while the ultimate view on any question has, of course, to be taken by Parliament, it does not follow that the processes preliminary to its decision must necessarily emanate from or be co-extensive with parliamentary machinery. For example, the detection of "policy" implications in the pricing practices of a Board involves a thorough comparison of pricing with cost structures; it is not in this part of the work that Parliament's competence lies but in taking a decision on the answers obtained from such analyses expertly and dis-passionately carried out by someone or other. Similarly in examining how far a policy decision—e.g., a price structure meant to achieve an income redistribution—has been effective, Parliament should be more concerned with arriving at the decision in the first place and with being shown, next, the extent to which the results corresponded with or deviated from the policy intentions, than with working out or probing into the practical details of the policy. When we consider

---

[1] Referring to the objection that "it is not perhaps the function of Parliament to intervene on the efficiency side to the extent which is envisaged by a Select Committee going into it", Herbert Morrison observed before the Select Com-mittee on Nationalized Industries in 1953, "I would die for Parliament—I have an enormous admiration for it—but I do not think it is the kind of body to which you could entrust this to the point of alteration of the actual management of a complex industrial concern." (Q. 479, Select Committee Report, 1953.)

The Select Committee on Nationalized Industries observed in April 1958 that their inquiry "was a case of laymen hearing technical evidence from one quarter only" (para. 4).

Lord Simon of Wythenshawe observed, "It is of great importance that Parlia-ment should realize that it is not competent to contribute anything whatever to the efficiency of the coal industry, whereas it may, if it interferes too much, cause serious inconvenience and contribute a good deal to the inefficiency of the industry." (*The Boards of Nationalized Industries*, p. 39.)

[2] The analogy of the Estimates Committee is not completely satisfactory in that the criteria of assessment are different in the case of the corporations and might call for thorough commercial investigations.

the object of ensuring the Minister's accountability for his own decisions, it is of course exclusively Parliament that should take the initiative.

There are, therefore, briefly three situations *vis-à-vis* Parliament, in which it has to play quite different roles in the context of ensuring public accountability. (a) Where the commercial efficiency of the Board is to be ensured, it would be best, on balance, for Parliament to set up other means which promote the efficient working of the corporation and indicate the level of efficiency from time to time. (b) Where policy issues are involved, it is desirable to provide for expert analyses necessary for forming views as a preliminary to value judgements which Parliament shall eventually make. This ensures freedom from bias at the stage of analysis. The area of decisions, with which Parliament may wish to concern itself, varies from industry to industry. In the case of some basic industries, Parliament may have definite views as regards the general level of prices, regional price structures and relative benefits to different consumer groups. Further, national interests, like self-sufficiency and employment policies, touch some industries more extensively than others. The point here is, not whether or to what extent Parliament should hold powers in these respects, but that, beyond or up to the stage where value judgements (whatever they are) are required, the analyses and the expert working should be left in outside hands. (c) Where the Minister's influence on the corporation is at issue, Parliament is naturally the body to be concerned. In broader terms, what is required is vigilance over the possibility of pressure being exerted on the corporation by reason of subjective decisions on the part of the Minister and the application of partisan policies of the party in power.

To sum up. Firstly, it is more essential for criteria of accountability to be established than the introduction of agencies for ensuring public accountability. For practical reasons, including practical politics,[1] particular agencies may appear to be necessary from time to time; and the members on the agencies may greatly influence the deliberations and conclusions with their personal views. The possible disadvantages of setting up certain agencies and of the members' undue subjectivity can be minimized by laying down adequate criteria for judging the corporations. Irrespective of their nature, the agencies would then limit themselves to establishing whether, to the extent

---

[1] For instance, the demand for a Select Committee was made, in Herbert Morrison's words, "from the Conservative side of the House when we were in office—and I think possibly by some of the Labour Members as well." (Q. 383, *op. cit.*)

that the Board has responsibility for decision, it has been efficient.

Secondly, the idea of setting up one agency or a few agencies to guard public accountability must be given up, if necessary, in favour of arrangements promoting continuously right managerial decisions on the part of the Board. After all, it would be a superior method to provide for a framework continuously making for efficiency as against the inception of investigatory or regulatory bodies; and where efficiency is guaranteed, the latter would be of small importance. Some of the means whereby a framework of efficiency could be promoted are as follows:

(a) The Acts or statutory instruments should be clearer on the relative roles of the Minister and the Boards, on the over-all financial targets of the Board, on the question of cross-subsidizations and on the broad considerations on which pricing should be based.[1] All ministerial influence on the Boards' actions should be made formal.

(b) The nationalized industry may be so organized as to provide for the following:

(i) A central organization, different in function from most of the present central boards, must be set up to discharge far less managerial functions than at present.[2] It should function as an adviser to the Minister, as a provider of external economies to the managerial units within the industry, and as an agency for several of the expert analyses necessary in the context of protecting the consumer interest, judging on the policy implications of Boards' decisions and setting up investment criteria. If properly evolved and worked, it could be a great pillar of public accountability.

(ii) The industry should subdivide itself, irrespective of the framework provided by statute, into optimum units, so that each unit—and therefore the industry as a whole—operates in the most economic manner.[3] If the optimum demarcations are carefully drawn up, these in themselves offer the best conditions of assessing cross-subsidizations, made possible by nation-wide or large regional corporations; for within the optimum area price differentials are in the nature of justifiable discrimination, whereas beyond they border on cross-subsidization.

(iii) There should be sufficient guarantee that the Board constantly is searching for improvements in internal organization. Three directions of action may be mentioned: (i) periodical consultations with management experts for suggestions regarding improvements in the

---

[1] See Chapter III.
[2] See Chapter IV.
[3] See Chapter IV.

methods of working; (ii) the setting up of a section to make un-announced tours of inspection with a view to recommending improvements;[1] and (iii) some organization analogous to the "common efficiency unit", suggested by Herbert Morrison. The actual steps to be taken in these directions by and large should be left to the Board; but there is the advantage that "the public knows it (the Board) has done something".[2] Since these refer to "internal" details, mainly relating to internal procedures and internal control or supervision, it is not necessary that all details of every finding should be given full publicity. In fact liability to full publicity might damp the Board's enthusiasm in referring matters to examination and criticism. At best the central organization of the new kind suggested may be given opportunity to make such investigations. Its broad conclusions should be published on a selective basis, if they are expected to have a bearing on wider questions of over-all organization rather than being merely detailed points of criticism.

(c) The consumer interest must be allowed to vindicate itself in the sense and on the lines described below.

Thirdly, all the agencies set up to improve or guarantee public accountability should work together consistently and in practice none should have an unfavourable effect on any of the four criteria of accountability and on the commercial efficiency of the corporation in particular.

### 3. *Some methods*

Let us examine some of the existing or suggested methods for improving the public accountability of a corporation and assess their effectiveness. It is not intended to make an exhaustive survey of all the devices, of which the arguments, on either side, are by now familiar, but to touch on such of them as involve a principle in the context of accountability.

(a) *Consumer Councils.* We shall limit the discussion to the role of the consumer bodies created under the Acts in ensuring the public accountability of the corporations. Our interest lies in the basic structural aspects of these bodies, and not in all their practical in-

[1] Analogy may be drawn to the idea given by Sir Edward Bridges, Permanent Secretary, the Treasury, when asked by the Select Committee in 1953 on the desirability of a "group of people with technical knowledge . . . operating on behalf of the Select Committee and perhaps going from one district to another district in the coalfields or from one power station to another . . . just looking in a mild kind of way for signs of inefficiency", that "they ought to be employed by the Boards themselves and not by the Select Committee". (Q. 900, Report, 1953.)

[2] Herbert Morrison, Q. 384, Select Committee, 1953.

adequacies as found today.[1] There are two reasons for establishing these bodies. Firstly, it is thought that the industry, being nationalized, must be amenable to the wishes of the consumers on grounds more or less analogous to those of democracy,[2] more surely than a private enterprise, working under an imperfect price mechanism, is; and secondly, being a monopoly, the nationalized industry calls for some public control which the consumer councils might provide. The emphasis on this motive is strengthened by two factors, viz., the exclusion of the nationalized industries from monopoly regulation under the Restrictive Trade Practices Act (except for transport still qualified by the Transport Tribunal), and the absence of any helpful rules in the Acts providing against monopoly practices in their multifarious forms, except for the good sense of the Boards and their interpretation of what practices are good or bad.

The former motive is political in its essentials and is derived from the view that every customer should be entitled to express his wish or grievance, not only because he consumes the product (for, subject to the monopoly elements in the industry, he could express himself, though only in the long run, through the price mechanism), but because he as a taxpayer is part-owner of the undertaking as well. Following up this idea, we are naturally led to two points. Firstly, the consumer bodies set up on this ground have limited use for the consumers as a whole or for the corporation (the producer). They may sometimes indicate consumer attitudes which cannot be

---

[1] The now familiar shortcomings of the consumer councils may be briefly mentioned as follows: (i) In general, they have a dual capacity: to "advise the administering authorities of certain reactions in the consuming public" and to "explain to that public the reasons for the authorities' actions"; and "experience indicates that they are difficult to combine". (J. A. G. Griffith, *Political Quarterly*, April–June 1950, p. 175.) (ii) They seem to be too closely linked with the Boards —through certain Board members sitting on the Councils, Board employees acting as Secretaries, Board premises being used as offices, Reports being included in the Board Reports and so on. Sometimes they give the impression of rubber-stamping Board decisions and whitewashing the Boards. (iii) They are not sufficiently known to all consumers. "The effectiveness of the machinery cannot be judged until . . . the public realize that there exists an independent authority specifically appointed to examine their complaints and empowered to make representations to the Board" and to the Minister in some cases. (Report of the South Eastern Council, Electricity.) (iv) The Councils have no research organization and cannot really argue with the Boards. (v) "The individual consumer is much too easily brushed aside, whether intentionally or not;" and "the present consumers' bodies are too inaccessible to the individual consumer"—e.g., coal and transport. (*The Political Quarterly*, April–June 1950, p. 178.)

[2] J. A. G. Griffith observes, "the public is more than an advisory committee; it is also more than a group of persons with individual complaints. The public is the body for whose benefit the industry is being run and the machinery is effective which persuades the public that this is so." p. 171.)

adequately inferred from the working of the price system.[1] Secondly, a variety of arrangements is possible as regards the organizational hierarchy of the consumer, the methods of consumer representation on the councils and the extent of rights that an individual consumer or a council at each level in the hierarchy should have,[2] without, however, losing sight of their effects on the organizational efficiency of the industry itself.[3] In other words, the composition of a regional or central council, the proportion of elected and nominated elements, the merits of local authority representation on the council and the proportion of domestic and industrial consumers—all these could be geared to the idea of how best the consumer may be represented. And there is no reason why the nature and composition of the consumer bodies should be identically the same for all the industries.

It is when we turn to the question of monopoly that the infinitely greater relevance of the consumer bodies to the issue of public accountability may be appreciated. The first question that arises is what they should be capable of achieving. In short, they should be in a position to challenge the managerial inefficiency of the industry, undue preference (not justified by given cost criteria), an excessive price level and any other monopoly practice like restricted output or irrational investment, and draw attention to policies containing elements of social policy. Further, the consumers as a whole should be strong enough to resist the possibility of the workers, through their bargaining power, forcing their claims against the interests of the consumers. There is an important asymmetry between the workers' claims, on the one side, and the consumers', on the other. Within a nationalized monopoly, the workers have a favourable combination of a political circumstance and an economic circumstance; their bargaining power rests partly on some shade of political

---

[1] Mary Stewart observes that "the chief function" of the Councils is "to ensure that the views of ordinary consumers will be expressed effectively to and considered seriously by the Boards" and not to work as "a natural enemy" or "teach the Boards how to do their work". (*Consumer Councils*, pp. 6–7.) Hugh Gaitskell himself emphasized that "the word 'consultative' is important. The Councils were not intended to be professional critics so much as advisory partners for the Boards. . . . In any efforts to perfect the machinery, do not let us make it so elaborate as to be altogether out of proportion to the job which has to be done." (*Ibid.*, Foreword.)

[2] Section 14 of the Electricity Act, 1957, empowers a consumer with a complaint to reach, in successive steps, the Electricity Council itself, under certain circumstances.

[3] For example, there is much to be said in favour of encouraging local complaints being disposed of at the local level, i.e., by discussion between the consumers concerned and the local managers of the industry. A local complaint successively reaching the Minister has its own adverse effects on the internal organization of the industry. Where, however, it involves a principle, this disadvantage may be outweighed.

support and partly on the eventual possibility of enhanced prices. On the other hand, the consumers' claims for lower prices have no easy chance of success, for, short of improved efficiency and reduced costs, they could succeed only at the expense of the taxpayers. For various reasons this is often the worse alternative for everyone in the end. Thus the normal process of wage determination within the industry's financial ability tends to be replaced by price determination depending on the success of wage claims.[1] Strongly organized consumer interest might be able to protest at this with some success, while, in its absence, the danger remains unchecked.

If the consumer bodies are able to take up these functions, more than half the battle of public accountability is won. For they can operate as an important check on the possible errors of monopoly behaviour on the part of the nationalized industries; and this in itself is an important element in the concept of public accountability as defined earlier. It is at this stage that the two ideas of representative organization and effective organization part company. For these functions to be discharged with the maximum success it is perhaps desirable to devise an organization which is small and competent, at the national level. There are traces of this idea in the widely appreciated need for "a small central research organization to advise council members on technical matters".[2] One of the concrete suggestions, made by P. Sargant Florence and H. Maddick,[3] is that a central consumer council should be established for all the fuel and transport industries,[4] composed of five to seven full-time members, the chairmen of regional councils and some twenty co-opted

---

[1] There has, however, been some emphasis recently in the field of Transport on the desirability of wage enhancements subject to the industry's financial ability, though the possibility of an increase in charges cannot be ruled out.

[2] Mary Stewart, *op. cit.*, p. 16.

[3] *The Political Quarterly*, July–September 1953.

[4] This differs from the central consumers' council suggested by J. A. G. Griffith. His scheme envisages county consumers' councils, a central consumers' council —about 150 strong, at the rate of one representing each county council—a cabinet Minister at the head representing consumer interests, county consumer Tribunals and a central consumers' Tribunal. ("The Voice of the Consumer", *The Political Quarterly*, April–June 1950.) He divides representations and complaints into three classes: general, particular and legal; and suggests that the last may be taken to law courts, the particular ones to county and central consumer Tribunals and the general ones to the county and central consumer councils. The "general" complaints he envisaged do not cover the fundamental issues of consumer interest raised above; and there is no way of raising or dealing with questions involving social policy or inter-consumer subsidization, either. The case for an "intelligence unit" to take charge of these matters still remains. His scheme is perhaps conducive to an effective representation of consumer complaints but does not provide for a thorough and competent investigation into the more basic points of consumer interest.

members; it should be equipped with a research unit. This, according to them, would cause the efficiency of the industry to be independently investigated and prices to be independently established, in due relation to cost; and it would improve the present position in which "the community lacks informed guardians capable of critically approving or suggesting alternatives to the Board's official proposals". They assume that this would give the community at large "some say in the choice" between alternative possibilities of policy decision.

If the central organization for the industry is revised as suggested elsewhere, it would go a long way in offering valuable information and undertaking expert analysis in relation to all the issues envisaged above by Sargant Florence and Maddick. This method would have two advantages, viz., that the central organization which, it may be recalled, is not to be a managerial body, would be able to offer all relevant data expertly analysed more economically than any other agency, since it maintains, in any case, competent staff for several other allied purposes; and that its access to the basic sources of information would necessarily be under more favourable conditions than the consumer council's, the latter being, in an extreme sense, a "hostile" body. But a central consumer council would still be necessary for two purposes: (i) all initiative cannot be left to the central organization in raising the points for investigation, and (ii) the presentation of a case from the impartially evolved analyses of the central organization ought to be made by the consumer body only either to the Board concerned or the Minister. It would, therefore, be necessary to set up a small central body, on behalf of the consumer councils covering the industry, and let it keep in touch with the central organization for the industry.

It is difficult to argue conclusively for one central consumer council for all the nationalized industries. There are at least three qualifications to such a course. Firstly, it does not preserve the necessary degree of homogeneity of consumer interest in tackling the problems of each individual industry and, in an extreme case, may leave every consumer positively dissatisfied. Secondly, contacts with the central organization of a nationalized industry would be more frank and effective, if attempted by a consumer council specifically set up for that industry. Thirdly, the practical efficacy of a common council naturally depends on the number of nationalized industries and the area of operations to be covered; whereas the individual council method is independent of this uncertain factor.

However, there can be a common research unit to help in the analysis of problems raised by any of the councils. Such a unit would be not only economical but capable of maintaining some uniformity of approach to the price and other problems faced by the consumers of the nationalized industries. The task of this unit tends to be functional and one mainly of expertise; and homogeneity of method would be a merit.

Finally it is a fact that there has been a tendency for consumers to take their grievances to their local Members of Parliament rather than to the consumer organizations set up under the Act.[1] It is difficult to say whether this is a temporary phase which would change with the gradual popularity or effectiveness of the consumer bodies. There is an implication of principle, however; a political medium of redress is preferred to an ordinary industrial method. If we should be faithful to the corporation principle of freedom from political interference, recourse to the consumer channels is to be encouraged, the more so as the public enterprises increase in number.

(b) *The Tribunal*.[2] Since the concept of public accountability includes provision against the abuse of monopoly power by the nationalized industry, the Tribunal, as a means of regulating its price policies and monopoly practices, gains relevance in the present discussion. It appears that this method of monopoly regulation (including the one under the Restrictive Trade Practices Act) was deliberately given up, except in the case of transport, in favour of consumer councils.[3] The choice of consumer councils, as against a Tribunal, would make little difference if the consumer councils are empowered to investigate price and other matters as thoroughly as monopoly regulation requires and if their findings have mandatory force. Earlier discussion has shown that the consumer councils have not been adequately designed to take charge of the basic elements of consumer interest—either in the short run or in the long run. It follows, therefore, that they should be revised in such a way that they would be able to study not only abuse of monopoly power but the most rational development of the industry in the long run.

The mere establishment of a Tribunal does not automatically improve the anti-monopoly machinery; nor does it *ipso facto* protect the consumer interest in the fundamental sense of the most rational working and development of the industry. There are two requisites to be satisfied, viz., (i) that cost should be made the basis of price

[1] The Electricity Consultative Council had only 39 complaints in 1956 for the whole of North of Scotland district, whereas one Member of Parliament alone, Sir David Robertson, had received more than "a couple of hundred" complaints in his "own constituency". (Q. 833, Report from the Select Committee on Nationalized Industries, 1957.)

[2] Here the reference is to a Tribunal of the kind of the Transport Tribunal.

[3] Herbert Morrison observed, "The establishment of such bodies in other cases" (i.e., Tribunals in other cases than transport) "was considered, but thought hardly appropriate." (*Government and Parliament*, p. 267.)

by law to be enforced[1] and (ii) that the necessary fact-finding and analytical machinery should be established. Given these two conditions, both the consumer councils and the Tribunal gain in utility and effectiveness; while in their absence they would have merely decorative value.

Let us see where exactly the Tribunal could be a superior agency, as compared with the consumer council of the revised type. There seem to be three situations in its favour. Firstly, the consumers of an industry may be heterogeneously composed, so that a representative organization is not easy to set up. Further, it may not be possible to arrive at an allocation of costs acceptable to all consumers. Under these conditions, the consumer organization tends to be of limited value, as it depends upon someone else to arbitrate or make decisions. (The example of coals of different qualities or different transport services, among which cost imputations are bound to be inexact, may be cited.) Secondly, in a situation where discrimination, justifiable in itself,[2] involves value judgements as between consumer A and consumer B, or as between region P and region Q—or where the Board could choose between A and B indifferently—no conclusive answer could be given by the consumer organization. The case for the Tribunal does not gain from the need to prevent cross-subsidizations. If these are not permitted under the Act and if the necessary facilities for establishing the cross-subsidizations, if any, are available—a necessary condition for the successful working of even a Tribunal—the consumer organization itself could work as effectively as the Tribunal. The third and last ground in support of a Tribunal is of fundamental importance. However efficient the consumer organization may be, its findings cannot have a mandatory force. Though the Board, by and large, would see advantage in accepting the findings resulting from the thorough analysis by the consumer organization, aided by the central organization for the industry, in the residual cases where it does not accept them, there arises a deadlock which must be referred to someone else, since the central organization—it may be recalled—does not and ought not to decide on the issue nor impose a decision on the Board. The Tribunal, on the other hand, may decide and, given the power, transmit the decision to the Board for implementation.

Unfortunately a more fundamental question arises at this stage. At the point where the rationale of a decision ceases to rest on factual

---

[1] Of course this presupposes a definition of cost and rules regarding the costs to be considered while fixing any particular price.

[2] In the present example, either A or B (either P or Q) may be favoured without placing any existing consumer or region at a disadvantage; but there is no conclusive ground *for the Board* for choosing A as against B (or P as against Q).

data, concerning costs, for example, where a single decision is not necessarily indicated and where, in other words, gross value judgements involving preference as between alternative eligibilities are involved, it is doubtful if any Tribunal, other than the Minister and Parliament, should be given final powers of decision and execution. It is partly on this ground that Gilbert Walker and Henry Maddick argue that the Transport Tribunal "as a final authority in rates and fares" is "obsolete and should go"; and they go on to urge that "the responsibilities for deciding policies, which affect the nation economically, strategically and socially, should no longer be laid on the Commission, but should be shouldered and discharged by the Minister subject to parliamentary control".[1] The role of the Tribunal, therefore, has a limited twofold purpose; it constitutes a court where any relevant point of view may be raised, as in the case of transport rates affecting different consumers differently and involving social or other broad economic considerations; and secondly, it can be employed as an expert agency for preparing conclusions or suggestions for the Minister or Parliament. This would be analogous to the prevailing procedure of the Monopoly Commission itself.

It is doubtful whether, beyond playing such a limited role, the Tribunal would be better for purposes of public accountability than an improved consumer organization, coupled with a revised central organization for the nationalized industry. The latter two would ensure continuous vigilance over the operations of the industry; while the Tribunal might concern itself with some cases in an *ad hoc* manner.

It is even more doubtful how far, under the present legislation, a Tribunal could be influenced by the industry's level of efficiency in recommending prices related to costs. Let us assume that an industry is managed inefficiently. It is morally right that the consumers ought not to be charged at the full level of costs; and under private enterprise governed by a regulatory commission the shareholders lose through low prices ordered by the commission—e.g., public utilities in the U.S.A. But under the financial arrangements of nationalization, low prices result in deficits which must be covered by subsidy, in view of the Treasury guarantee of capital issues; alternatively a reduction in the capitalization of the industry may be effected, consequently transferring the loss to the public exchequer. Attention to inefficiency is good as a means of exploring the prospect of lower costs (and prices); but where inefficiency continues, the Tribunal can do little about it while regulating prices, for the simple reason that either of the two consequences shown above raises broader questions

[1] G. Walker and H. Maddick, "Responsibility for Transport", *Political Quarterly*, July–September 1952, p. 234.

and calls for (political) decisions by Parliament. Obviously the Tribunal has no role to play in this respect, except in presenting expert data and inferences, as suggested earlier. If we examine in this light the suitability of a Tribunal to ensure "the right of the consumers as a whole to be charged not more than cost, to have the efficiency of the undertaking independently investigated, and to have the general level of charges independently established,"[1] the inadequacy of the Tribunal as a final authority in these matters is apparent.

(c) *Periodical inquiry.* One of the suggestions made by Herbert Morrison is to set up an inquiry composed of "competent business people", "ordinary good citizens" and "parliamentarians", "once in a matter of about seven years" on the lines of the B.B.C. Inquiry. He thought it was "a better tribunal . . . than is a Select Committee of Parliament".[2] It is desirable to distinguish between the case for an occasional inquiry whenever Parliament requires details about an industry or of certain of its operations, or when it contemplates a change in the organization of the industry, and the case for a periodical inquiry as a method of ensuring public accountability. In the former case the merits of the inquiry are clearer; and in fact an inquiry of that nature could be set up in connection with any private industry, as in the case of railways, gas or electricity before nationalization. Being a post-mortem examination, the periodical inquiry can only disclose past facts, comment on the merits of past decisions, and offer opinions on past managerial behaviour. Its influence on the efficiency of decisions as they are made is little, except for the fact that the Board is constantly aware of an impending examination at some future date. It is difficult to say whether this by itself prompts them to exhibit the utmost efficiency, more than the fact that the Board members are charged with public responsibility. In any case, its influence is both-sided; it stimulates efficiency as probably as it chills it by encouraging the "play-safe" mentality.

The inquiry would be of great use if it is followed by legislative or ministerial action indicating to the Board the lines on which to act in certain situations discovered from past experience. To some extent the Herbert inquiry into the electricity supply industry may be cited as an example. However, some of the Committee's findings—e.g., those relating to self-financing, rural electrification and self-insurance —are still not followed by changes in the Act or by ministerial directions.

---

[1] W. A. Lewis suggests that "the prices of every public corporation should, in its Acts, be made subject to the scrutiny of an independent tribunal (not necessarily a different one for each corporation)". "Price Policy of Public Corporations", *Problems of Nationalized Industry*, edited by W. A. Robson, p. 194.

[2] Q. 384, Select Committee, 1953.

The inquiry method is more useful when we turn to its relevance, not in promoting the commercial efficiency of the Board, but in (i) discovering the policy implications of the Board's major decisions, (ii) examining, if necessary, the consistency of Board policies with the over-all policies of the Government, (iii) verifying how far the Government's policy directions to the Board have achieved, through the practical media of Board policies, the intentions with which they were given, and (iv) making any other relevant inquiries into matters reflecting national interest, as defined or described by the Government at the time of the inquiry. It may be recalled that the central organization, as suggested in the present discussion, would cover most of these points from day to day and would, therefore, help in ensuring public accountability. Yet it may be desirable to institute a periodical check-up in respect of questions involving considerations broader than commercial efficiency, so that all sections of the community can, by their representation on the Committee, participate in the expression of views. The central organization of the industry would be available to help the Committee with its expertise in the matters under inquiry. The danger of outsiders looking over the Board's shoulders is limited by the fact that the inquiry is focused on matters involving social policies.

(d) *The Select Committee.* Before we discuss the role of a Parliamentary Select Committee in ensuring public accountability, brief reference may be made to the comparison sometimes made between Parliament and a shareholders' meeting.[1] The analogy is only partial;[2] and there are vital differences which seriously qualify the inference that Parliament ought to function in the same way as the shareholders do in controlling a company. Firstly, Parliament is political in composition and representative of all interests in the country, with the result that it lacks the simple criterion of size of profit, by which generally shareholders are guided. Secondly, Members of Parliament bear no personal risk as a result of decisions taken by or imposed on corporations, unlike the shareholders of a company. The result is that their attitudes could affect at random the consumer, the worker and the taxpayer. In other words, we lack precise yardsticks by which the consequences of a decision are to be measured. Lastly, Parliament does not have the power directly to appoint or dismiss a Board member; and it is not impossible that even the present

---

[1] For example, Sir Herbert Williams of the Select Committee mentioned that "a select committee might be a sort of shareholders' meeting". (Q. 824, Select Committee, 1953.)

[2] For a discussion on this point, see D. N. Chester, "Management and Accountability in the Nationalized Industries", *Public Administration*, Spring 1952.

system of appointments may be improved in course of time so that the Minister's influence—or political influence, to put it broadly—would be of formal and nominal importance, except in special cases. In fact one may generalize that, if public enterprise is based on the idea that the private shareholder of the controlling type is not necessary for the efficiency of the industry today, the corporation is based strictly on the further idea that control from the shareholder of the political type is not conducive to its success.

The setting up of the Select Committee was recommended in order to provide "for such an enlargement of the field of parliamentary accountability as will provide the House of Commons with the information which it rightly requires without, in obtaining the information, interfering with or jeopardizing the efficiency of the Nationalized Industries".[1] The problems raised by the working of a Committee of this nature are partly practical and partly those of principle.

On practical grounds the following comments may be made. (i) The Committee, by the nature of its composition, cannot devote enough attention to consider all the nationalized industries every year. In practice there have been only two Reports, since the Committee was first set up in 1955. The first of these referred to two Electricity Boards—the North of Scotland Hydro-Electricity Board and the South of Scotland Electricity Board, and the other one related to the National Coal Board. At this rate the Committee can comment on particular Boards only at random and once in a series of years; and the element of continuity in the concept of parliamentary accountability is missing. (ii) If it is accepted that the Members of Parliament are not necessarily efficiency experts[2] and that an assessment of the industry's efficiency, the central theme of all accountability, is a function of meticulous examination into policies and details of performance, the unsuitability of the Committee, if for this purpose, would be self-evident. (iii) The questions which the Committee investigated seem to be quite sweeping, some touching on policy and some on detail, some referring to technical matters—for example, pumped storage. There is no consistent attempt to examine either policy or efficiency. It would be possible

---

[1] Report from the Select Committee, 1953.

[2] The Select Committee spent a day (20th of March, 1957) in asking A. T. K. Grant, an Under-Secretary in charge of Trade and Industry Division of the Treasury, to "suggest any particular line that you would think would be useful for us to ask Mr. Johnston (Chairman, North of Scotland Hydro-Electric Board) to prepare himself for". (Q. 170, Report.)

The Select Committee observed "in much of the inquiry, it was a case of laymen hearing technical evidence from one quarter only". (Report, April, 1958.)

for a capable Board to interest the Committee sufficiently without the Committee ever being able to discover anything of value on its efficiency or public responsibilities, or for the Committee members to learn at random any point that interests them politically or for any other reason.

The usefulness of the Committee is even more qualified on grounds of principle. Firstly, the Committee's findings are of partial value in the adjudgement of the Board's efficiency, for they do not touch, nor are based on, the several ingredients that make up the concept of accountability, as earlier defined. This by itself would be no serious disadvantage if it were not for the fact that the findings gain currency and amount to a prejudgement of a complicated issue. The point may be illustrated by reference to the 1957 Select Committee's conclusion, regarding the North of Scotland Hydro-Electric Board's rural electrification, that its activities are not "throwing an unfair burden on one group of its consumers". In support were advanced three arguments[1] which unfortunately do not lead to that conclusion on grounds of economic logic. It is legitimate for Parliament to acquiesce in any price structure it deems desirable; but it would be unfortunate to draw somewhat misleading conclusions on the intrinsic nature of a prevailing price structure. Were such incomprehensive findings to be unfavourable to the Boards, they are sure to suffer incalculable harm in prestige and internal staff discipline. Secondly, the very idea of the Select Committee is based on unsure foundations, unless it is meant to be a purely information agency. If it is to "elucidate . . . deep problems of policy",[2] a better device would be for Members of Parliament to question the Minister on his responsibility for major policy decisions taken by the Board, discuss them, express opinions on them and urge the Minister to give effect to their approved lines of thought. This of course presupposes clarity between the decisional areas of the Board and the Minister, which is lacking today. It appears from the Committee's Report of 1957 that it wanted to compensate this lack by cross-examining the Departmental and the Board spokesmen for information regarding the respective responsi-

---

[1] "Your Committee considered this criticism at some length, but were unconvinced by it. The tariffs charged by the Board throughout its area are by no means unduly high—they are, for instance, lower than those charged in Southern England. . . . Secondly, a large part of the Board's income is in any case derived from the sale of electricity to the South of Scotland . . . , so that, if anyone is subsidizing the development of electrification in the Highlands, it could be claimed that the consumers in South Scotland are among them. Finally, it seems probable that the large towns, if supplied only by their own steam or diesel power stations, would have to pay more for their electricity than they do now." (Report, p. ix.)

[2] Hugh Molson, Q. 317, Select Committee, 1953.

bility of the Ministry and the Boards for certain decisions. It is doubtful if, in the long run, this is the correct way of achieving a desirable object. With regard to questions other than those of policy, the Committee is a less defensible proposition; for in the words of Lord Reith, it "was in effect a negation of what Parliament deliberately did in setting it (the corporation) up".[1] Lastly, direct questioning of Boards and Departments by members of Parliament might sometimes leave the Boards and the Departments in a confused state and, in any case, force them to a "play-safe" attitude. Or they may raise the constitutional issue of whether they should answer certain questions. There are already traces of this in the Report of 1957.[2]

Perhaps the best way of understanding the limitations of the Select Committee is by noticing "parliamentary accountability" as the underlying purpose envisaged by the Committee that recommended its formation in 1953. There are two points to note in this connection. Direct parliamentary accountability, apart from the Reports by Boards and the liability of Ministers to be questioned, is inherently not part of the concept of a public corporation. Secondly, the real content of public accountability is more comprehensive than that of parliamentary accountability, which at one end could be a synonym for improved information and in any case excludes all those constituent ideas of managerial efficiency, with which the Committee is not expected to concern itself. The problem of ensuring public accountability, therefore, remains even after a Select Committee starts functioning; and its best contribution would be the negative one of not impinging on the commercial efficiency of the corporation Boards.

(e) *Certain broad arrangements.* So far we have discussed some of the major specific devices suggested for increasing the public accountability of the corporations. If we carefully scan through the literature on the subject, we discover in some suggestions an under-

---

[1] Lord Reith, Q. 593, Select Committee, 1953. He continued, "Parliament passed a sort of self-denying ordinance taking from itself the right of direct interference, as with Government Departments. Unless there is to be a revision of attitude, I would have thought it was contrary to the principle of what was done that you should set up a committee."

Herbert Morrison observed, "I think it follows that, if questions cannot be put about it (management), it would be difficult to justify a Select Committee investigating it." (Q. 501, Select Committee, 1953.)

[2] Pressed for detailed information on the relative responsibilities of the Ministry and the Board for changes in coal prices, J. Latham, Deputy Chairman of the Board, was compelled to say, "I would be only too happy to answer this or any other question if the Minister said it was the right thing to do, or if you directed me to do so, but I would be reluctant to do it without having that guidance." (Q. 1122, Report from the Select Committee, 1957.)

current of thought favouring certain over-all developments that ensure public accountability. Mention may be made of three suggestions—(i) an over-all consumer council (by P. Sargant Florence and Henry Maddick), (ii) a common efficiency unit (by Herbert Morrison) and (iii) a Minister of Public Corporations or Nationalized Industries (by Lord Reith). (To the last category belongs J. A. G. Griffith's suggestion of a Minister (without portfolio) representing the consumers.)[1] At the outset these proposals seem to emanate from different angles, though underlying them is the need for some common over-all arrangements in the field of public enterprise. The over-all consumer council for all nationalized industries could concern itself with pricing and other questions of common policy relevant to every one of the corporations. For example, the exercise of monopoly power, efficiency-cost-price relationships, discrimination and cross-subsidization, investment criteria, etc., are aspects regarding which the approach to the particular problems of one nationalized industry need not greatly differ in principle from that of another. If the suggested Council is not found practicable, this incidental merit is nevertheless worth realizing by whatever other means is practicable —maybe through a common intelligence forum of the central councils for the different industries. The common efficiency unit—"the product of all Boards" to be used as "industrial consultants" in solving "economic", "costing", or "managerial" problems which the Board "could not solve itself"[2]—could provide for the necessary exchange of views in tackling problems commonly affecting large, monopolistic, public enterprises organized as corporations. In fact it could concern itself with the additional function, not contemplated by Herbert Morrison, of watching and deliberating, from the industries' managerial viewpoint, on such constitutional issues as the propriety of a parliamentary question, ministerial influence on the Board's working and the Select Committee's investigations which, by general understanding, ought not to cover managerial aspects nor affect the Boards' commercial efficiency. The Minister for Public Corporations could look into constitutional questions of "when to intervene" in a corporation's affairs, what constitutes a managerial aspect as different from a Ministerial responsibility, etc., and could greatly improve the prevailing position in which "degree of accountability varied; attitudes of Ministers varied; the positions that the corporation boards had made for themselves varied; and there were other variations great and small; the differences had become shocking, anyway odd."[3] Lord Reith, however, did not suggest "a hard

---

[1] *The Political Quarterly*, April–June 1950.

[2] Herbert Morrison, Q. 384, Select Committee, 1953.

[3] Lord Reith, Q. 593, Select Committee, 1953.

uniformity"; yet he pointed at the need of "rationalizing and order-ing what is unrational and disorderly today".[1] There is great truth in Lord Reith's comment, which is corroborated by others in certain specific matters;[2] and whether a Ministry is set up or not it would be a desirable improvement to set up some machinery on the Govern-ment's side for looking into these matters from the constitutional angle, with a view to building up consistent long-run traditions and practices, free from the emotional appeal of a specific issue at a given moment of time. There seems to be some support for this suggestion when one looks at the way in which corporation laws are being standardized in certain directions in the U.S.A. and Canada.

Public enterprise as a relatively recent form of industrial organiza-tion, considering the scale of its coverage, has its own problems, as distinct from those of private enterprise; and the organization of a public enterprise through the corporation medium raises additional (and sometimes fine) problems. The greatest need is of course for the synthesis of economic concepts as reflected in industrial efficiency with political concepts as reflected in the democratic desire for control. In tackling, if not in resolving, it, every step in the direction of a general framework, which, however, must be separately evolved from the different major directions, is welcome. Whether a common consumer council, a common efficiency unit or a Ministry of Public Corporations is set up or not, some machinery giving effect to the underlying ideas of each of these must be constructed in order to achieve consistency in the public accountability concepts of the different industries.

(f) Finally there is the view that efficiency will take care of itself, if the Board is left to itself without being bothered by external con-trol. There is an element of truth in this contention, viz., that, when the Board feels free from the fear of someone looking "over its shoulders" all the time,[3] it could exhibit the utmost commercial

---

[1] Lord Reith, Q. 615, Q. 649, Select Committee, 1953.

[2] For example, Sir John Mellor observed, with reference to the Parliamentary question that, "after a very careful examination of these questions which he (the Minister) answered and those he refused to answer, I have been unable to discover any underlying distinction at all." The Minister proceeded "apparently according to his taste and fancy" (443/45).

Further, see Rt. Hon. Sir R. Manningham-Buller's (Attorney-General) evi-dence before the Select Committee, regarding the varying practices in different Ministries on matters engaging the Minister's responsibility. (Qs. 11 and 12.)

[3] Herbert Morrison observed, "on the whole, I want the Board to take care of themselves." (Q. 418, Select Committee, 1953.)

Lord Reith felt "frightened of a select committee" because "it would develop into control". (Q. 670.)

Lord Heyworth said, "The more you can make this into autonomous units I think the better chance there is for success." (Q. 754.)

initiative in its functions. As Lord Citrine observed, with reference to the suggestion of an efficiency unit, "there would be a strong tendency on the part of every body to plan for safety. This would lead to a disinclination to accept responsibility, and once started such a process might easily shatter the initiative of people otherwise ready to accept responsibility. A 'safety-first' mentality could easily become the most deadly enemy of efficient administration."[1]

However, there are three arguments qualifying this contention. Firstly, all Boards might not always display the highest initiative possible, since neither competitive forces nor public vigilance compels them to be zealous about it; and the good intentions of "being left to themselves" may be inadequately realized in practice. Secondly, the elements that go to make up the concept of accountability are such, as seen from earlier discussion, that there is a positive need for some degree of public intervention which prevents certain consequences of Board action and promotes certain results from external decision; and this need is independent of the degree of efficiency that the Board may attain. Lastly, there is the practical, though semipolitical, fact, which cannot be disregarded in evolving the institutional arrangements under nationalization, viz., that the public and Parliament must have positive means of satisfying themselves that the results expected of the Boards, are produced, notwithstanding the Boards' lack of direct pecuniary interest in the results. As long as the satisfaction of this legitimate desire is consistent with the conditions conducive to the Board's efficiency, there is much to be gained by setting up the necessary machinery. The more important question is what this machinery should be and what its effects are on the Boards' efficiency—a question dealt with earlier in this section.

It is, on the whole, desirable to provide for the conditions best suited to efficient performance by the corporations and introduce specific *ad hoc* agencies of public intervention in regard to matters of social or non-commercial policy. The latter by themselves would ill-serve the object of commercial efficiency; while sheer insistence on commercial efficiency would not always guarantee the over-all social interests. There should be an appropriate balance between the commercial and the social interests.

## 4. *The company form*

Let us finally discuss the special aspects of public accountability as applied to government enterprise through the medium of joint

[1] Lord Citrine, "Problems of Nationalized Industries", *Public Administration*, Winter 1951, pp. 325–6.

stock companies. This method has been applied extensively in Italy and to a significant extent in India and may form an important part of the future nationalization philosophy of the Labour Party in Britain.

The company is a legal entity, like a corporation, but is not formed by a special Act, unlike a corporation. Though it is government-owned, it is not a department of Government; and there can, therefore, constitutionally be no direct means of governmental or Ministerial intervention in its working, unless the Articles of Association permit of it. However, the requisite of public accountability is paramount in the case of the government-owned companies, for three reasons, viz.: (i) the investments are public; (ii) the managerial Boards are publicly appointed and have no direct pecuniary interest;[1] and (iii) social consequences might follow from the Boards' actions in certain situations—almost the same reasons as apply to the public corporations.

However, the question is more complicated than in the case of the corporation. For, the picture of government participation through the company medium is a heterogeneous one, as illustrated by Italy,[2] and can be presented under the following classification.

(a) The Government may own fully all the companies in an industry; or it may be a single-company industry, the Government owning the company—e.g., the Hindustan Shipyard of India; or the Government may have a majority holding in each company in the industry. The common feature of all these variations is that competitive tests are absent in the fields of pricing, profit accumulation, efficiency promotion, inter-consumer subsidization and the exercise of monopoly power with social consequences. The problems are almost analogous to those met in the case of the corporations, except for the fact that possibly there is a larger number of autonomous units under the company method. The fourfold concept of public accountability envisaged in Section 1 of this chapter holds good here too.

(b) The second situation is one in which the Government's hold-

---

[1] If the Companies Act requires the directors to hold qualification shares, the directors of the government companies may hold the minimum number of shares to satisfy the formality.

[2] In some of the public enterprises in Italy, "the State is the sole owner. In others the State owns only a majority, or even a minority, of the stock. In still others, the State owns such a small proportion of the stock that it cannot be said to possess effective control". The percentage of total national employment, for which the IRI accounted in 1954, varied from industry to industry—e.g., 13% in engineering, 49% in iron and steel and shipping, 38% in public utilities and broadcasting, 70% in telephones and 30% in banks. (Einaudi, Bye and Rossi, *Nationalization in France and Italy*, p. 243 and p. 205.)

ing is limited to a little more than a bare majority in the industry. In whatever ways this is done, a substantial share remains in private hands and, unless the Government abuses its position for exercising absolute control over the entire industry, the private sector has a part to play. In fact it is to ensure this that often a strong plea for mixed enterprise is made—e.g., in Italy.[1] If the arrangement is preferred in order to facilitate flexibility in managerial behaviour and promote competitive ideas and initiative in the conduct of the industry, it would be necessary to ensure that the Government (and the Government-nominated directors) do not reduce the effectiveness of the private sector within the industry. It is in maintaining a judicious balance between government majority on the one side and the role of private initiative on the other that the success of the mixed enterprise system depends. This, therefore, constitutes an important element in assessing the managerial behaviour of the government sector.[2]

(c) Where the Government's share in an industry is too low to give it monopoly powers, even if every company owned is fully owned, the desired concept of accountability is more qualified than in the above cases and amounts merely to the concept of bare commercial efficiency. Enough competitive forces are preserved within the industry; and the best that the government units can hope to achieve is competitive success. The concern of Parliament is, therefore, limited to this aspect.

(d) The last situation sets the least problem—where government participation takes the shape of partial ownership of some companies at random, without any consistent principle regarding the Government's share in each company or in the industry as a whole. (A position like this could develop if *any* shares are accepted towards settlement of death duties, or if the Government implements welfare policies resulting in its participation to some extent in industrial

---

[1] Ernesto Rossi observes, with reference to the IRI method of mixed enterprise in Italy, "the supporters of the mixed system maintain that it enables the State to draw upon the experience of private businessmen, who are members of the boards of directors of the mixed corporations; that it possesses a flexibility in the management of affairs which leads to successful operation; and that it draws upon private resources for the supply of needed capital funds." (*Ibid.*, pp. 243–4).

[2] Reference may be made to the allegations made by the British independent airlines of the activities of the B.E.A. and the B.O.A.C. (Of course these are corporations and not companies, discussed above.) Examples may be cited of Aquila Airways desiring to use flying-boats and the Eagle Aviation's application for permission to run London–Venice flights. It is alleged by the independent airlines that the interest of the Air Corporations stood in their way of securing the permission.

flotations in underdeveloped regions or regions suffering from acute unemployment.) Here the Government-nominated directors have in general a passive role to play; and in certain of the latter cases where government participation is dictated by broader social considerations, the directors' actions would be heavily under the influence of government policy.

The third and the fourth situations differ from the other two in freeing the Government-nominees on directoral boards from having to make all-industry decisions and perhaps from the very exercise of monopoly power. To that extent the canon of accountability to which they are subject is simpler.

We do not have adequate experience of the company type of public enterprise to be able to make systematic inferences on the question of public accountability; for the arrangements as regards ownership, management, appointments to boards, and accounts and audit vary greatly from case to case. A few points may, however, be made on theoretical grounds.

Firstly, the content of the concept of public accountability depends on the structure of government participation in the industry concerned. The important question is: what degree of monopoly does it imply over the industry concerned or over the management of the companies concerned? To put it in another way, what are the purposes of government participation in a given situation? The purposes may range over the following: (i) the object of income for the exchequer —this may be explicitly expressed or negatively construed in the case of holdings not inspired by any other specific purpose—e.g., shares received in payment of duties; (ii) to influence the industry's development, employment and location policies; or to prevent monopoly practices against consumers; (iii) to employ the company as an instrument of economic or social policy—e.g., to foster economic activity as an employment measure; and (iv) unclear reasons—e.g., an emergency take-over in a situation of bad industrial relations or shares acquired as tax receipts. The main point to draw from the great variety of motives and structures of government participation in companies is that there can be no hard and fast rule regarding the content of public accountability. There are always border cases that ought really to be managed departmentally or as corporations; and the fact that company status is conferred on them need not preclude the application of canons appropriate to departmental administration or corporation organization as the case may be.

Secondly, the flexibility of managerial arrangements possible with the company form is not an unmixed blessing, as shown by experience. A clear answer on the function of the Government nominees is the minimum requisite in placing the company method on a sound basis. The answer is clear in the case of the department as well as in the case of the corporation, at least in theory; whereas the Government's day-to-day relationship with companies and its powers of intervention in their functioning are as yet too poorly defined. The arrangements so far at work have disclosed the following possibilities: (i) the company is declared to be a legal entity different from the Government and the Government absolves itself of responsibility for its operations—"a fraud on the Constitution" as observed by the Auditor-General of India; (ii) "the civil servants who today are running private or mixed corporations are not answerable for their activities before any administrative tribunal, not to mention Parliament;"[1] (iii) the Government-nominees act as the Minister or department wishes[2] and yet Parliament cannot discuss what are described as the autonomous decisions of the companies. The situation is complicated to no small extent by two factors: (i) the inclusion of civil servants in directorates and (ii) the mixture, in some proportion, of Government-nominees and the private directors on the boards.

(i) Civil servants by habit carry out the department's policies and look to the senior colleagues in the department for advice which is treated as direction[3]—as happened even with the autonomous Life Insurance Corporation in the infamous Mundhra episode in India.[4] The practice is more certain to take place if the civil servants act in a dual capacity—both in the department and on the directorates; and in any case their behaviour is in general designed to please those on whom they depend for advancement in their careers. The questions needing clarification are, therefore, whether the Government nominees are expected to be subject to constant government influence and whether the behaviour expected of the civil servant nominees is the same in this respect as that of the outsiders nominated. There must be clear provision for discovering the extent of government influence on the nominees, so that, if necessary, it could be discussed

[1] *Nationalization in France and Italy*, p. 244.

[2] Einaudi observes, with reference to the IRI in Italy, that "a majority of the members of the board of directors are merely representatives of various government departments, appointed by the heads of those departments and removable at will by them. Thus the Boards stand exposed to the twin influences of politicians and of bureaucracy, the latter asserting itself to an increasing degree as the former becomes more confused." (*Ibid.*, p. 28.)

[3] With reference to the company method in South-East Asia, A. H. Hanson observes, "where official departmental representatives sit on the Board of Directors, as is invariably the case, they are sometimes afraid of acting in an individual capacity and inclined to refer most points of importance to their ministerial chiefs." (*Public Enterprise*, p. 410.)

[4] Reference has already been made to this case in the first Chapter.

by Parliament. Unlike a corporation, the company is not governed by a specific Act; the Articles of Association should be so framed as to define the relations between the Government and the government company, must contain clear provisions on this matter and lay down the channels of government influence. Over and above this, *ad hoc* directions by the Minister ought to be issued whenever necessary. In other words, it is desirable that no influence should be exerted by the Government, without its being known to the public; and the company's results must not be judged without full knowledge of the government influence underlying them. Companies which facilitate government or ministerial intervention without public notice or challenge are worse as a medium of public enterprise than both the department and the corporation.

(ii) The exact purpose of a mixed board is not clear in many cases; and it is doubtful if the Government nominees allow the private contingent on the board to show initiative. The more the Government's influence on its nominees, the less important the private directors. The mixed board might be an excuse for pretending that the company is an autonomous body, though in fact it does not act as one. The only way of obtaining the benefits of mixed managerial talent is by effectively freeing the government directors from constant government influence.

With the increasing number of government companies, it has been realized in India that they ought to be brought under stricter public control than has existed so far. But the question as regards the nature and extent of direct government control still awaits the right answer; and it is equally important to decide on these aspects of the company method. Recently some positive steps were taken in the direction of public control; provisions specifically relating to the government companies were included in the Indian Companies Act— Sections 617 to 620. These relate to auditing in the main and empower the Government to appoint the auditor on the recommendation of the Comptroller and Auditor-General of India, who lays down the methods of audit and could, besides, "conduct a supplementary or test audit".

If accounting audit is not confused with efficiency audit and if the connotation of efficiency and public accountability is rightly understood, it is difficult to regard these provisions as the most appropriate measures for ensuring either the efficiency or the public accountability of the companies. To free commercial enterprises from such audit routines is one of the basic objects of the public corporation. It is not clear why the government companies should be subjected to them. That public funds are involved is no argument; this applies equally to corporations. These provisions may have the

140

positive effect of reducing the financial behaviour of government companies to the level of departments and the negative effect of misleading one to believe that full provision has been made for public control.

# CHAPTER VI

# ALLOCATION OF CAPITAL TO PUBLIC ENTERPRISE

THE success of a public enterprise consists partly in the conditions determining its appropriate capacity in the long run. It should work at a capacity justified by consumer preference; and no more (or less) resources should be drawn into it than are remunerated comparably with the factors employed in other economic activities. While the ideal is simple, the problem of allocating capital is complex with regard to the public enterprises, because the criteria of allocation are complex.

Though the Herbert Committee on Electricity opined that "in the nature of things the use of capital cannot be as strictly or as closely guided by economic considerations as is the case in private industry",[1] their recommendations on capital expenditure emphasized the need for economic criteria. Perhaps the need is all the greater in a situation where economic criteria might get superseded by other considerations.

The purpose of the present discussion is to suggest profitability as the basic criterion of investment.[2] The complications surrounding the concept of profitability and the sense in which it should be applied to nation-wide State monopolies will be examined; and some methods of preserving profitability as a helpful criterion will be proposed. Comments will be made on the question of self-financing. We shall then consider criteria other than profitability and examine the condi-

---

[1] Report of the Committee of Inquiry into the Electricity Supply Industry, 1956, para. 347.

[2] It is not proposed to enter into an elaborate discussion of pricing and output under public enterprise, on which plentiful literature is available. The present Chapter has the limited purpose of discussing investment criteria for practical policy. Reference may be made to the following literature on the subject. A. P. Lerner, "Status and dynamics in socialist economics", *Economic Journal*, June 1937; J. E. Meade and J. M. Fleming, "Price and output policy of State enterprise" (a symposium), *Economic Journal*, December 1944; R. H. Coase, "The marginal cost controversy", *Economica*, August 1946, "The economics of uniform pricing systems", *Manchester School*, September 1947, *Economic Journal*, April 1945; A. M. Henderson, "The pricing of public utility undertakings", *Manchester School*, 1947, "Prices and profits in State enterprises", *Review of Economic Studies*, Vol. XVI (1) 1948–49; T. Wilson, *Economic Journal*, December 1945; W. A. Lewis, *Economica*, November 1946; H. Norris, *Economica*, February 1947; *Crossland*, Oxford Economic Papers, January 1950; A. P. Lerner, *The Economics of Control*, Ch. 15, 16; I. M. D. Little, *A Critique of Welfare Economics*.

tions under which they should qualify the profitability criterion. It is not suggested that the profitability criterion is simple and accurate but that, by and large, it should be the guiding principle.

## 1. *The problem under mixed enterprise*

Let us start with the case of mixed enterprise—i.e., an industry in which the government undertakings form a part. This is, however, not the prevailing situation in Britain, though in countries like Italy and India it is of importance. In an area of mixed enterprise, the role of relative profitability as an investment criterion for the nationalized undertakings is dependent on the relative importance of the private sector. Where the private undertakings account for a significant proportion of the industry's output, it is likely that prices result from the play of market forces. The Government, it may be assumed, does not depress the prices specially and cover the deficits of the public units by means of subsidies. If this happened, the private units would gradually leave the field, unless they could compete through increased efficiency, or, alternatively, unless they were also subsidized by the Government; and the hypothesis of mixed enterprise becomes invalid.

As long as mixed enterprise operates successfully, profitability remains the chief criterion of investment. Even if the government units remain neutral to the criterion, i.e., even if they do not expand under conditions of high profits and contract under conditions of low profits, the private sector would increase its investments when profit rates are high and decrease them when profits are low. In this way the right kind of adjustments in aggregate capacity are brought about by the market mechanism operating through prices and profits.

It is assumed for the sake of this argument that the government units do not operate under permanent cost advantages over the private units. If they did, their prices would become too competitive with those of private units which gradually would have to leave the field. Where the government units enjoy a permanent advantage like lower interest charges, other things remaining the same, their profits are higher than those of the private units; and, unless the profits are partly made over to the general exchequer, they lead to (i) a reduction in prices, (ii) a re-investment or (iii) higher returns to factors— wages, in particular. In the first two cases, the forces are set in motion for the private units to leave the field; and the problem eventually takes the shape of total public enterprise in the field. In the last case the government units once again tend to work at the same cost levels as the private units; and the earlier description of mixed enterprise holds good.

143

## 2. *The problem under public enterprise*

The problem of allocation of resources undergoes a change under conditions of public enterprise—i.e., in industries where the whole or nearly the whole activity is in the hands of the Government. Fundamentally there are four reasons for the change.

(a) *Ideological*. The notion gains wide currency that, once an industry is nationalized, its development must be subject to the deliberate decisions of the Government. These are naturally a super-imposition on the impersonal decisions of the market characteristic of private enterprise.[1] Basically this rests on the new outlook of planning which forms part of the economic policies of many governments today to some degree or other. It is generally believed that the regulation of allocation in the public sector is a convenient means of achieving certain results of employment and business activity. Where private enterprise lags behind the Government's exhortation in a particular direction, the Government is tempted to act in the public sector in a compensating manner.

(b) *Political*. An extensive public sector presents an opportunity for the party in power to manipulate the investment programmes with an eye on the consequent political advantages to the party. To the extent that this motive deviates from the over-all national interests of employment policy, it is objectionable on economic grounds.

(c) *Decision making*. The managers of nationalized industries initiate investment decisions under conditions that do not provide for the rigorous tests of the market, unlike those in competitive industries. Two points of interest ensue. Firstly, how can we be certain that their decisions are the appropriate ones, if there is a lack of accepted criteria on which the decisions are framed or could be adjudged? Secondly, to the extent that the criteria of decision are vague and deviate from the market tests, is it right that the managers' decisions should be taken as final? It is for these reasons that, in the Select Committee's words, "instead of having to undergo the discipline of the market to obtain their money, they (the National Coal Board) have to convince the Ministry and the Treasury that the money will be well spent."[2]

(d) *Legal*. The Nationalization Acts lay down that the investment programmes should be settled in consultation with the Minister and the Treasury. In exercising this function the Minister, who is answerable to the political body, viz., Parliament, is guided by factors which

---

[1] Of course the impersonality of decisions is qualified by the monopoly elements prevailing in many fields of private enterprise.

[2] Report from the Select Committee on Nationalized Industries, April 1958, para. 25.

are not exclusively economic in nature. In fact what is contemplated under this arrangement is an appropriate compromise between the economic criteria of allocation, which the Boards may present, and the non-economic criteria that the Government may have in view. This is far from simple. The former are already qualified by the conditions under which the Boards are able to initiate their investment plans, and the latter are indefinite. The question of allocation of resources among the public enterprises, therefore, turns out to be a complicated one.

In the early stages of nationalization, it is usual for allocation decisions to be taken in the light of exigencies prevailing at the time of, or calling for, nationalization. The under-maintenance of the British railways and coal-mines may be cited to illustrate the circumstances conducive to allocation decisions on grounds of long-felt needs.[1] Physical scarcities likewise appear to be an overriding factor underlying allocations—e.g., the electricity industry. (This is an outdated consideration in Great Britain at the moment.) Such initial requirements may be justified even on strictly economic grounds and elaborate proof, which is not attempted, may not be necessary. However, as these requirements are met, further allocations should be made to depend on definitive criteria in order to preserve some order in the development of the public enterprises as between themselves and in relation to the rest of the economy.[2] The need will be greater as the area of the public sector expands and the variety of the public enterprises increases. It is equally necessary to test from time to time whether a given scale of investment in an industry is in need of contraction in view of its changing market conditions. This consideration gains in importance from the asymmetry between expansion and contraction in one sense: contraction is not so commonly thought of, nor tests so carefully applied, as in the case of expansion.

However, the case for profitability as a criterion of allocation under public enterprise depends on two questions. Firstly, is the profit test a reliable test under conditions of monopolistic public enterprise? Secondly, assuming that it is a reliable test, is it a conclusive test under nationalization?

At this stage it is useful to note a few preliminary points regarding

---

[1] Even in these cases, where the need for investments meant to improve efficiency is generally recognized, each individual item of capital expenditure ought to be judged on the criterion of its relative worthwhileness.

[2] For example, the Select Committee on Nationalized Industries observed, "the Treasury approval is qualified by the belief that 'a closer sense of calculation will come in' once enough coal is being mined; and your Committee believe that, even now, there should be no possibility of output being sought without the most thorough of financial tests." (Report, April 1958, para. 32.)

the criterion of profitability. If the nationalized industry makes a profit from a region, product or plant, the *prima facie* indication is that further outlays in that direction are justified. Larger outputs may go with lower prices and, in the process, we may reach a stage where high profits cease to repeat themselves. Now there are two complications. Firstly, the limits of demand may have been reached in the region concerned; and past profit does not necessarily indicate the desirability of further investment. Here it is essentially a question of control over monopoly pricing; and the managers of the nationalized undertaking are in need of external guidance. Secondly, the undertaking may commence investment in another direction where the returns will be low, on the ground that the average will be sufficient in view of the profits from the former line. This is a wrong assessment, for the test of investment must rest on the expected profitability in the case in question; and inter-regional or inter-market subsidizations are not justified, except when made by parliamentary decision.

The profitability criterion may therefore be understood in terms of the specific investment in question; and past profit is a criterion only in the case of an investment in the area of the past profit.

The term "over-allocation" (or "under-allocation") will be employed in the discussion to denote a larger (or smaller) allocation than is justified on the criterion of profitability. The term "autonomous allocation" is used in the sense of an allocation analogous to what is indicated by the market forces, and the term "non-autonomous allocation" implies an allocation made on grounds other than the profitability criterion.

### 3. *Is profitability a reliable test?*

Is the concept of profitability definitive and reliable for purposes of allocation under conditions of public enterprise operating as a monopoly? Resource allocation is a relative problem, in the sense that an allocation to an industry can be assessed as proper, too great or too small, in relation to that of another activity on some common criterion of profitability or returns. It is well known that the aim should be to equalize the marginal returns or marginal profitability everywhere. It is, therefore, necessary as a first step to be sure of the comparability of profitability as between the different industries concerned. In other words, the question to be considered is whether profitability as indicated by the profit figures is homogeneous as between private and public enterprise, as between public enterprises themselves, and over time in the case of a given public enterprise. The claims of profitability as an allocation criterion are qualified to the extent that such homogeneity is lacking.

The forces operating on profitability are different as between private and public enterprises. The content of cost varies in the two cases, with the result that the meaning of profit differs in the two cases. Pricing policies may be dissimilar and the impact of external influence on managerial behaviour unequal, so that the criterion of profitability tends to have dissimilar purport in the two cases. To the extent that private enterprise is qualified by such public regulation as brings its cost and price conditions nearer to those of public enterprise, or, alternatively, to the extent that public enterprise is permitted such autonomy of management as entitles it to act as enlightened private enterprise, the comparability of their respective profit results improves. Or else, the profit criterion operates as a criterion of limited usefulness, when the economic system is considered as a whole.

Even as between different public enterprises, the term profit is not uniform in its content. They are under the impact of different methods of compensation. Their methods of securing capital vary and they adopt different policies of self-financing. The profit as first calculated does not hold the same meaning in every case. The profit test is reliable to the extent that, in the case of each industry, the profit is the result of autonomous behaviour, significantly dependent on cost and demand conditions.

It is, on the whole, easier to equate the background conditions for the profit criterion being rendered reliable as between the nationalized industries than between private and public enterprise. A few suggestions will be made in that direction in the course of the discussion. At this stage we shall examine the factors that complicate the concept of profitability under public enterprise.

(a) *The concept of profit.* If profit is understood as the difference between revenues and costs, the interest of the analysis shifts to the costs on the one hand, and the pricing policy on the other. Let us first inquire into those cost factors that operate with a distinctive force in the case of public enterprise.

The first of these is the cost of capital. This is under two influences. On the one hand, Treasury guarantee[1] keeps down the cost of obtaining capital. The advantage is bound to be significant for capital-intensive industries. At the higher rates of interest at which these industries might have secured capital in the market, the cost of capital would have been higher. (In the case of transport a very high rate might have had to be offered.) The low level of costs as shown in the books does not reflect the real value of the factors acquired by these industries. The same factors get higher returns elsewhere; that is,

---

[1] The Herbert Report, para. 351.

consumers demand their use elsewhere. In order to prove that these factors are no less required in these industries, it would be necessary to write up the cost of capital acquired, in the light of the prevailing market conditions, even though the method of Treasury guarantee is continued. In the absence of such a policy, there follows too high an allocation to the nationalized industries. (The Herbert Committee on Electricity raised this question and observed that the desirability of going direct to the market was common to all the nationalized industries.)[1] That nationalization is meant to offer this advantage (of low prices and large outputs) is an unsound argument; for it simply implies that the opportunities of securing higher returns from the use of factors elsewhere are ignored and that the consumers of the products of the nationalized industries are chosen for a special price benefit as against the others. It is not clear whether this is based on Parliament's decision to subsidize the former consumers at the expense of the latter. In the case of public enterprises competing with industries left in private hands, there is the positive disadvantage of the former industries developing at the expense of the latter, not because consumers show their preference, but because they are offered lower prices due to the cost economy under the head of interest charges.

The method of Treasury advances or Treasury guarantees keeps the fixed cost of capital low, in the sense that the payments to be made to the holders of the stock are low. If, however, the cost is written up in the books of the nationalized industry, the difference between this inflated figure and the actual payment to stockholders accrues to the Government for general use. Yet this is not in the nature of a tax on the products concerned. Nor does it particularly restrict the outputs, though it does not encourage expansion of the nationalized industries. (This suggestion has to be considered along with the discussion in the next section referring to the social returns expected to accrue from the expansion of certain basic industries.)

The other influence on the cost of capital is derived from the compensation paid at the time of "take-over". This sets, as it were, "the rate base" which, together with the rate of interest, determines the cost of capital. Two questions arise: (i) does the amount of compensation represent the real value of capital employed and is it related to its earning power? (ii) Has the method of compensation been the same for all the nationalized industries? It is difficult to answer either question in the affirmative with reference to the nationalized industries in Britain. For example, the working results of transport amply prove that there was excessive compensation—not in moral terms but in terms of earning capacity. Compensations not linked with the

[1] The Herbert Report, para. 351.

earning power of the industries may be termed as the result of political decision. These may be excessive (e.g., where the new interest charges exceed the former owners' profits) or, alternatively, niggardly (as in the case of the Renault motor factory in France which was "confiscated"). In either case the rate base is the product of political decision. The question arises to what extent the consumer, as against the taxpayer, should bear the impact of it. In the case of over-compensation, the best course would be to transfer the excessive element to the national debt; while in the case of under-compensation, the capital figure of the industry may be written up. The latter in fact would favourably affect the figure of national debt. Thus the taxpayers may be made to bear the consequences of political decisions on compensation and the consumers relieved of them. On balance, the excess-compensations and under-compensations might cancel out, in so far as the taxpayer is concerned, though this really depends on the actual compensations paid in the several cases; while the factors used are properly valued, in so far as the consumer is concerned, in the sense that they are costed out at the market rates of securing the capital. This policy has much to commend particularly where the consumers are not a bulk sample of the taxpayers, and where the industry in question is closely competitive with another industry either in the public sector or in the private sector—e.g., electricity and gas, or railways and road haulage. For, in these two cases, it is not a matter of indifference as to whether the burden is borne by the consumers or the taxpayers.

Unfortunately the solution is not so easy as it appears at the outset. What is the proper basis for capital reconstruction, when an attempt is made to vary the amount of compensation? Obviously the basis cannot be a revaluation of the properties used, for this has no reference to their usefulness in the industry from the consumers' point of view. If earning power is chosen as the basis, is this to be assessed in terms of the results at the time of take-over and on the assumption of the continuance of the same pricing policies? This has the advantage of being a clear basis; but its acceptance is politically unlikely; for if the compensation turns out to have been an over-compensation, the Government responsible for it would be criticized. Alternatively, should credit be given for the economies of nationalization and the new possibilities of monopoly pricing, when earning power is evaluated? The assessment would now be a matter of guess-work, unless it is undertaken a few years after nationalization. In the latter case, of course, the fresh complication arises of the managers' ability or indifference to reach targets which vary between different political parties and consumers.

Thus the practical answer is bound to be somewhat arbitrary. Some capital reorganization[1] is, however, necessary in those cases where the new capital charges can be met only by an extraordinary exercise of monopoly power by the public enterprise. Basically, the clash is between the consumer's interest and the taxpayer's.

The second complication in the field of costs concerns the social costs which cover, in the words of K. William Kapp, "all direct and indirect losses suffered by third persons or the general public as a result of private economic activities." These cover "the social losses of production for which neither law nor custom has as yet established an adequate responsibility of the individual production".[2]

Obviously there is a difference between private and public enterprise, viz., that certain social costs are directly borne by the latter, while the incidence on private enterprise depends on the tax system devised for the purpose. Even among public enterprises, there is no equality of the social cost burden. Certain social costs are borne at Board discretion—e.g., social privileges for workmen or officers;[3] while certain others are borne at random dependent upon governmental decision—e.g., non-closure of a coal-pit or the continuation of an unremunerative railway service. To the extent that the costs of the industries are differently affected by such Board or government decisions, profit ceases to be a homogeneous criterion of allocation.

Let us consider some specific items of social cost borne by the public enterprises.

(i) The nationalized industries are generally provided with some kind of a consumer organization. The cost of organizing consumer opinion in this way is a new cost. Further, *if* the consumer organizations tend, in effect, to discharge the functions of monopoly control to some degree, the cost of such monopoly control again becomes a special burden on the nationalized industry. (The cost of consumer organizations is, of course, not a considerable element in their total cost structure.)

As against this, certain economies are derived. For example, advertising expenditures can be scaled down, partly because of organized two-way information services between the industry and the consumers. (In fact there is an agitation against mutually destructive advertising by electricity and gas.) Besides, the consumer organization may help the managers of the industry in deciding on the right risks and expansion programmes.

[1] I. M. D. Little suggests "a capital re-organization at the time of take-over". (*A Critique of Welfare Economics*, p. 206.)

[2] K. W. Kapp, *The Social Costs of Private Enterprise*, p. 13.

[3] Up to a certain point employee welfare and amenities are an economic cost for the business unit, private or public. But beyond this point they are in the nature of a social cost and the magnitude may vary arbitrarily from one unit to another.

It is a question of fact whether, on the whole, the cost burdens or the cost advantages are higher. It is true that private enterprise itself spends heavily on market research and on developing good relations with the consumers. It is difficult, therefore, to compare the actual costs borne by public and private enterprise under the head of consumer organization. In any case, it is possible that in the future some kind of consumer organization will develop in private industry; and the costs of such organization may, in some way, have to come from the industry itself.

(ii) Similar are the costs of central planning. Every nationalized industry maintains a central organization, the like of which may or may not exist in every private industry. Here again there is a tendency to establish some kind of a planning nucleus at the centre, for the sake of industrial planning in the private sector. The Iron and Steel Board, set up under the Iron and Steel Act, 1953, is a good example. Its costs are met by the industry itself.

(iii) Public enterprises are more surely influenced by public policy on industrial location. On grounds of public health, military strategy and local employment opportunities, certain units may be located in places where their costs of working are relatively high. Government regulation on industrial location may not be equally effective in the case of private enterprise, in both preventing undesirable locations and encouraging desirable locations. The managers of nationalized industries, on the other hand, develop the habit of interpreting the over-all interests that the Government has in mind and often are provided with positive advice by the Government in this respect. To the extent that their costs settle at a higher level than in the case of private enterprise, for this reason, their profits are not conceptually homogeneous with those of the latter.

(iv) Public enterprises do not always take a purely commercial view of their employment policies. For example, retrenchment is undertaken less zealously than under private enterprise. The point is illustrated by the comments of the Herbert Committee that the Electricity Boards have not retired incompetent men quickly enough and that the problem of redundancy has not been faced squarely;[1] apart from this, there is the possibility of increasing the workmen's privileges out of proportion to what happens under private enterprise. Thus the profit figure amounts to an understatement.

(v) The greatest difference in the cost structures of private and

[1] The Select Committee on Nationalized Industries referred to the importance of transferring the miners to another colliery before a colliery was closed, lest they should be "lost to the industry". "It is in addition necessary to consider the social impact which the closing of a pit may have on the surrounding area." (Report, April 1958, para. 19.)

151

public enterprise arises from the relative difficulty of contraction in the case of public enterprise.The closure of unremunerative mines or railway lines may be cited as an example. Examples are known, though not in Britain, of undertakings having been nationalized because they were being closed down and because they would lead to unemployment.[1] Part of the explanation rests on the notion of external benefit flowing from public enterprises of a basic nature; while more fundamentally it depends on the political reactions to contraction of capacity. To the extent that the public enterprise consists of redundant capacity the cost structure is affected adversely and the actual aggregate profit is smaller than the possible profit. What is worse, the case for contraction is concealed by the way in which aggregate profit figures are available or calculated. Whereas private enterprise is always anxious to search out redundancies with a view to reorganization, public enterprises have far less interest in doing so.

(vi) Finally the statutory obligation imposed on certain public enterprises (e.g., Transport, to repay capital in 90 years) imposes on them an item of cost not relevant to most private enterprises. This implies a burden on the present consumers for the sake of the future consumers. There is, however, a point of greater interest at this stage. By raising the target of recoverable costs, it lowers the figure of profit in the early years when the annual repayment provision exceeds the interest on the repayments effected to date. During this period the profitability of the industry appears to be lower than it would have been in the absence of this extraneous consideration. If its profitability is taken as a criterion of investment, allocations would be relatively low. If, on the other hand, the appropriation for capital repayment is not necessary, additional allocations are possible as far as they are justified by the actual rates of profit. Is it right, one may ask, that the current development of the industry should be starved for the sake of a subsidy to its future consumers? The question is analogous to that of self-financing which will be discussed in the Appendix at the end of this Chapter.

From the above discussion it is concluded that profits cannot be taken as a guide to allocation unless there prevails greater similarity in the forces operating on profits in public and private enterprise and then as between the public enterprises themselves. The method of attaining the similarity is threefold. Firstly, adjustments should be made to certain cost items under public enterprise, e.g., the cost of capital. It would be enough to do this once and initially. Secondly, allowances should be made for the effects of public policy specially

---

[1] E.g., Pignone, a machine tool firm in Italy, was nationalized for this reason.

imposed on public enterprise. These are, of course, difficult to make, and yet necessary for the additional purpose of judging the commercial behaviour of the enterprise. No accuracy can be claimed for the quantitative estimates of social costs[1] and the decision should lie with Parliament in the ultimate analysis. Thirdly, the obligations of private enterprise towards social costs, once the latter are decided upon, should be made as effective and substantial as in the case of public enterprise. Of course we would be up against the difficulty of defining the social costs for which responsibility should be placed on private undertakings. An illustration may be given. The establishment of a new unit may have unfavourable repercussions on an existing unit. The workers in the latter cannot be absorbed in the new unit if their skills are not suited to the production techniques of the new unit. If the new unit is a public enterprise, they may be absorbed, nevertheless; whereas a private unit is not likely to do so. Now, is the cost of unemployment to be reckoned an item of social cost to be imposed on the new unit? Or, should the new private unit be required to absorb these workers?

(b) *Monopoly pricing.* The size of the profit is influenced by the pricing policy of the undertaking. Under conditions of State monopoly the output and price policy can be "managed" in many ways. Let us start with the assumption that the managers adopt a profit-maximizing behaviour. (This, however, is not the prevailing tendency in Britain.) Two results may follow: (i) high profits, and (ii) inter-regional discriminations. Let us examine their relationship with the question of allocation.

(i) High profits generally go with restricted outputs. The moral, therefore, is that the profits should be brought down through additional allocations resulting in expanded outputs. Thus to make profit an allocation criterion is the surest way of bringing down high prices under conditions of State monopoly. It is not suggested, however, that prices should be so reduced as to reduce profits to the zero level. The question of what profit should be aimed at is discussed later.

There is, however, a complicating circumstance. High profits might encourage higher payments to the factors of production. Now the

---

[1] As K. W. Kapp observes, "the final determination of the magnitude of social costs of production is ultimately a matter of social evaluation; i.e., the magnitude of the social costs depends upon the importance which organized society attributes to both the tangible and the intangible values involved" (*op. cit.*, p. 21).

H. B. Chenery says that, in calculating the social marginal productivity of capital, the social cost criterion "is less likely to be useful as a rule of thumb because it is more difficult to calculate" than the other criteria like balance of payments and capital intensity. ("The Application of Investment Criteria", *The Quarterly Journal of Economics*, 1953, p. 76.)

costs themselves are higher and the final figure of profit may once again seem to be lower. The case for allocating resources becomes weaker, and the output does not expand. For example, higher wages would be demanded if the monopoly made high profits; in fact this has been an argument against the usefulness of a rise in coal prices.[1] So, it may be argued, high profits may not long retain their character but get dissipated in higher costs. Though the prices really reflect the consumer's desire for more output it may not be forthcoming under these conditions. This is a real difficulty. The basic question is whether the factors of production, the employees in particular, in the nationalized industries should cost (or be paid) more than those elsewhere. As long as the employees' bargaining power and closed-shop techniques enable them to demand higher rewards, there is an under-allocation for a given level of prices, as compared with private enterprise. (In broader terms, this is analogous to managerial or organizational inefficiencies resulting in higher costs and factor use for a given output.)

(ii) The more important comment on the profit criterion under large-scale monopoly is that the aggregate profit has no meaning as an allocation criterion, in view of the very large size of the organization. The over-all profit is the result of aggregating the results of individual parts and ought not to be taken as a guide to allocation. The problem is not essentially one of increasing the aggregate output of the industry on the strength of some consumers subsidizing the others, but of adjusting the output of the individual units into which the industry may be divided on optimal grounds.[2] The latter alone ensures the best utilization of factors; and the total costs at which the aggregate output is made available are likely to be the lowest. Allocation for a whole industry has no meaning except in terms of allocation at those points in the industry where it is called for. For example, an Electricity Board may make an over-all profit of 12 per cent. This is the weighted average of individual figures relating to the Sub-Areas or Districts, of which some may have made far higher profits while some may have made deficits. It is in the former regions that more resources are justified and not in the latter. If we go by the over-all figure and allocate resources to the Board as a whole, the resources may be employed even in the deficit regions. This is not the real purpose of the profit criterion. A practical case in point

---

[1] One half of the Ridley Committee on National Fuel Policy saw that, in raising prices to the level of marginal costs, one of the difficulties would be that "the miners would consider that these apparent profits justified corresponding wage increases". (Para. 67 of the Report, 1952.)

[2] It may be remembered that the question of social returns from an individual allocation programme is kept outside the present discussion.

is the National Coal Board's discussion of the purely average yield "expected from the investments planned for the coming year".[1]

The real test of allocation should, therefore, be applied locally. The profitability of each optimum unit must be considered as the main determinant of resource flow into that unit; and the aggregate allocation to the industry should simply result from the aggregation of these figures. This is of special significance in the case of "extensive" industries like electricity, gas and transport, which must install equipment in the markets served.

It is true that, even if the Board of a nationalized industry goes to the capital market without Treasury guarantee, it secures the resources on the strength of its over-all profitability.[2] To this extent the cost of capital depends, not on the expected results of investment at the point it goes to, but on the over-all profit position of the Board. It is, therefore, necessary to require the Board to apply the profitability criterion to every specific investment before it bids for capital in the market on its over-all strength. This is one of the major problems posed by nationalization.

We shall now relax the assumption, implicit in the above discussion, of purposeful behaviour on the part of the managers towards a specified or maximum profit. At present the pricing policies are not definitive in the sense that there are no given rules of pricing. They may not be consistent over time or as between the different national-

---

[1] Report from the Select Committee on Nationalized Industries, April 1958, para. 26.

In some cases, it is difficult to decide which units of the industry are the deficit ones deserving contraction but no further allocations, under conditions of a managed price policy. Coal pits serve as a good example. Other things being equal, e.g., social considerations apart, the best answer would be to concentrate on output at the less costly pits and contract output at the more costly ones, so that the total demand, at a given price, is met. Where it is physically impossible to expand the output at the low-cost pits so that the total demand at the given price is met, it is necessary to raise the output at the high-cost pits if it is desired to meet the whole demand. It would be logical, in this case, to raise the price so that the costs of the high-cost pits are met; and the profits of the other pits would rise correspondingly. If, however, it is decided to keep the price low, the high-cost pits turn out to be unprofitable. In other words, two social decisions of importance are involved here: firstly, that no consumer shall pay for coal higher than the given price; and secondly, that the markets that have to be served by the high-cost pits, on consideration of transport costs, shall not pay higher prices than the others (corresponding to the higher costs of those pits). Now the concept of a deficit-pit is arbitrary; and it becomes definitive only when pricing is not so managed as in this example.

[2] The nationalized industries in Britain have been financed by Treasury advances, rather than by borrowings on the market, since 1956. The original tenure of period during which this arrangement should work was extended for at least another year in February 1958.

ized industries. There are no statutory targets of profit or principles of pricing which they are obliged to keep in view. The only condition is that in the long run the industry should not be other than self-sufficient. Any figure of profit is permissible; and the managers have no definite reason to work towards one figure as against another. Further, they may adopt any pattern of price discrimination, since they are not provided with rules as to price-cost relationships. They begin to interpret the public good according to their own lights and follow pricing policies that are casual compared with maximization policies. For example, three units may adopt three pricing methods—uniform prices in one case and different patterns of discrimination in the other two cases. Let us assume that the resulting outputs are the same but the profits are dissimilar. None of the managers can be termed inefficient, since there is no given test of efficiency in terms of profit. In the absence of guidance, each thinks that his policy is the most desirable one. The three units would then be eligible for different allocations if these were based on the profit criterion. In fact the unequal profits do not reflect the consumers' preferences so much as the random behaviour of the managers concerned. Any of the three policies might have suited every unit equally well. Given uniform rules of pricing, or on applying one manager's policy to all the units, the profits in the three cases may have been equal and the eligibility to allocation the same for the three units.

Another illustration is found in a situation where an outlay seems to be unremunerative under uniform pricing, as the cost curve runs above the demand curve right through. Now one manager may choose to give it up; and there is correspondingly a lack of allocation to the industry in the region concerned. Whereas, another manager may elect to adopt a policy of discriminatory pricing such that the investment becomes possible on the test of profitability. The disparity in the investment decisions in the two cases is the product of the absence of clear pricing rules for the managers. There ought to be some known uniformity in the methods of earning the price proceeds. (Incidentally, industries in which discriminatory pricing is not possible or easy tend to derive relatively low allocations in comparison with the industries which can operate discriminatory pricing.)

It is, therefore, necessary, if the economic criterion of profit is to hold good, to promote clarity on pricing policy—e.g., the maximum profit for a given output, or the maximum output for a given profit. A ceiling of profit may be stipulated, if desired, and the managers allowed to work objectively within the ceiling. Profits would then reflect consumer preferences, taking, as in any situation of business management, the managerial efficiency as given.

As suggested earlier, the profit target should be provided for each individual optimum unit within the industry, so that no over-allocation or under-allocation takes place at any point within the industry. Where over-allocations or under-allocations and inter-unit subsidizations are contemplated by the Government, it would be preferable, at the instance of the Government, to stipulate varying profit targets in the different regions. For example, if a high profit rate is laid down as the aim in a region, investments in that region are bound to be such as do not jeopardize that rate; whereas, if a low profit rate is stipulated as the aim in another region, investments can take place despite the low profit rate recorded. Such peculiarities in investment decision, it may be repeated, ought to be the result of external decision only.

Where a capacity which is chronically under-utilized may be construed as "over-capacity", i.e., where a structural change has occurred against it, it is necessary to scale down the capital figure so as to relieve the consumers from the burden of financial charges traceable to the under-utilized capacity. Since it is in the nature of an investment risk, the owner—i.e., the taxpayer in this case—ought to bear it. In private enterprise working under competition this takes place all the time. In other words, the capital concerned should be written off by a transfer to national debt. Otherwise, there arises inter-consumer subsidization, which is analogous to the taxation of some consumers for the benefit of others. (It is assumed that there are profits elsewhere in the system.) Alternatively, the Government may pay an annual subsidy to the industry in respect of the capacity kept in use. Now the consumers elsewhere do not bear the burden of it.

To anticipate a later argument, this is not a plea against any resource allocation in a region where the profit criterion does not justify it, though other considerations might. The present argument is simply that investment decisions should be autonomous, in the absence of clear justification on consideration of grounds external to the industry in question, and that nationalization by itself should not alter radically the principle of a unit's expansion on its own merits.

(c) *Government policy.* The criterion of profit is, further, qualified by the fact that the profit may have already been under the influence of government policy on prices and on income redistribution. Curious results might follow if no adjustment were made for such influence and the profits of the different nationalized industries taken to indicate their investment priorities. Certain instances of external influence are given below.

(i) The working results of the public enterprises may have been influenced by the price-freeze policy of the Government. This applies especially to basic industries and public utilities. For example, many

Gas and Electricity Boards abstained from raising their prices in 1957 under the weight of government policy. As another example of ministerial influence on prices it may be mentioned that, in the case of coal, "on one occasion in 1953, a proposed price increase to reduce a deficit was overruled by the Minister of Fuel and Power."[1] The Select Committee on Nationalized Industries observed that "in the last analysis it is the Minister of Power who says what the public must pay for coal".[2]

The profits resulting from such restrictive influences on prices may compare unfavourably with the profits of another industry which is not under the same kind of external influence.[3] The former industry might receive a relatively low allocation of resources if we proceeded on the criterion of recorded profits. This is probably a wrong decision, since the consumers, if given the opportunity of bidding for the product, might have indicated the extent of their preference for an expansion of the output and for additional allocations. Relying on the force of this argument, the Government may deduce the justification for investment and proceed to allocate resources to the industry, despite the low profits. The real difficulty, however, is that we do not know how much the allocation should be. It becomes a matter of judgement, since there are no given criteria of profitability. It would be the product of political decision, the Government deciding what prices the consumers must pay for a certain product. The nearest

---

[1] Report from the Select Committee on Nationalized Industries, April 1958, para. 78.

[2] *Ibid.*, para. 80. Also see para. 87: "Of the ten applications for a price increase made by the Board, on four occasions the amount granted was less than requested, and one application was refused outright; on five occasions the increase began later than the date asked for."

"The increases (in price) which have been made and the dates on which they have been made have not always been those which were proposed by the National Coal Board." (Deputy Chairman, National Coal Board, Q. 1105, Report, 1957.)

Incidentally, it may be noted that the policy of coal pricing on the basis of average cost, under conditions of higher and rising marginal cost, is the product of government policy. It is wasteful to add to the inputs an amount which is not fully realized through the price of the resulting output. If market forces have a free play this would not happen; and the price settles at a level equivalent to the cost at which the marginal output is produced. If the National Coal Board were allowed to operate as a commercial undertaking, it might work towards such a pricing principle. But there would result higher prices and lower outputs than at present. The Government do not seem to approve of these results. To this extent the use of resources in the coal industry is heavily under the influence of government policy.

[3] For example, the competitors of the National Coal Board, "including the other nationalized power industries", are not tied down to any agreement analogous to the "Gentleman's Agreement" applicable to the National Coal Board.

case in point is the coal industry. The prices are controlled by the Minister; the National Coal Board is not permitted to adopt a pricing policy on commercial lines; deficits are recorded; yet large investments are taking place. It is impossible to say to what extent the investments are justified as long as prices and profits are so "managed" as at present.

(ii) The Government might treat a public enterprise as a means of indirect taxation. Departmental enterprises almost automatically serve this purpose. Even in those cases where a separate budget is permitted for such enterprises, an arrangement may be made for a certain surplus being made over to the Government—e.g., the British Post Office and the Indian Railways. The British corporations do not have to surrender any part of their profits to the Government. There are corporations elsewhere in the world, which under statute have to do so—e.g., in India. Wherever the Government expects an income from the public enterprise, it is difficult to decide what part of the profit is realized as a tax revenue and, therefore, ought not to be taken as a criterion of fresh investment, unless the amount expected as a tax revenue is fixed, at least roughly. Then the profit rate at which the industry should work would be known clearly to be the sum of interest charges, reserve appropriations and the indirect taxation. If profits rise above that figure, additional allocations may be made; and once again profitability at some known level revives as a criterion. It is true that other industries, which are not treated as sources of indirect tax revenue for the Government, become eligible for larger allocations in spite of their lower profit rates. But this is the result of the Government's decision, implicit in the indirect tax policy, that the former industry shall be relatively restricted. Where the industry in question serves an inelastic demand, there would be few effects on output; and the question of allocation is not greatly complicated. In the main it is the questions of income distribution that arise here.

This part of the discussion may now be concluded. The profitability criterion turns out to be crude and inadequate, unless the necessary adjustments are made for the special influences at work on the profitability of each nationalized industry. The adjustments on the side of costs are easier, on the whole, than those on the pricing side. The difficulty in the latter case is at a minimum if there exists uniform managerial behaviour, say, towards the goal of profit maximization. In the absence of it, which is the real situation, the actual profits earned reflect managed pricing policies involving widely varying price-cost relationships in different industries. If the Government has no specific pattern of these relationships in mind, on grounds of income distribution, the price-cost relationships could be made uni-

159

form among the nationalized industries by statutory or ministerial direction; and arbitrary managerial discretion in this respect may be kept at a minimum. The resulting profits would then indicate consumer preference and serve as an investment criterion for the industry concerned. But where the Government influences the price-cost relationships of different industries differently, perhaps on grounds of income distribution or of external economies, the actual profitability of an industry does not have the value of indicating its relative profitability *vis-à-vis* the other industries for investment purposes. The problem of resource allocation, which really is a relative problem, becomes difficult under these conditions. Once again we come back to the evaluation of the desirable level of investment in the absence of an objective criterion like profitability. There can be no answer except in terms of the benefit to consumers which the Government wishes the industry to offer.

The argument presented here is not that every nationalized industry must expand to the point of zero profit. After providing for all costs including proper depreciation and payments of purchase taxes or "royalties", if any, and after setting aside funds for reserves for ensuring interest payments, it may aim at some degree of self-financing. The limits of self-financing must be clear, however. (The question of self-financing is discussed in the Appendix to this Chapter.)[1]

### 4. *Is profitability a conclusive test?*

Let us now assume that the profitability criterion is reliable. It implies that when the profit is high investment is desirable, and *vice versa*. This ensures the movement of resources appropriately with the consumer's wishes as expressed through prices. If, however, there are other grounds which the investors and the consumers, acting in individual groups, cannot fully appreciate and act upon, and if these grounds appear to the Government to justify, on broad national considerations, a modification of the autonomous resource flows, profit clearly cannot be the final test. Whether the enterprise is private or public makes no difference to the argument. In fact the plea for a tax or a subsidy in cases where, respectively, the social returns are lower or higher than the private returns, is basically a plea for

---

[1] There is no room for the argument that the nationalized industries may work at high profits which may be made over to the general exchequer; for under the British Acts of Nationalization this is not permitted. On the other hand, if the general exchequer expects an income from the nationalized industries, appropriate taxes may be levied on the products concerned or "royalties" or "excise duties" charged, as suggested by some in the case of coal; and these would then form part of the recoverable cost of the industries. Our argument is not affected.

the evaluation of the over-all effects of an economic activity.[1] Thus the public interest, as interpreted by the Government, should qualify the direct profit test of allocation.

There is, however, a twofold convenience in the case of public, as compared with private, enterprise. Firstly, it can be so organized that its investment policies automatically take into account interests broader than direct profit. The departmentally organized public enterprises generally belong to this category. This is equally possible even with the public corporations. For example, a large corporation can easily substitute over-all profit criteria for specific investment criteria. Whether this is right or whether it should take place as automatically as it does is another question,[2] and has been discussed earlier.

Secondly, public enterprises offer themselves as media of compensatory policies, in the sense of policies that compensate for what private enterprise does not do or does inadequately, despite the Government's exhortation. Here the reference is only to aggregate economic policies such as the employment policy; and the justification for certain allocations to a public enterprise may not necessarily be in terms of the needs of the industry in question but may depend on the need to compensate for the deficiencies of private enterprise in a total employment plan.

In many countries the public sector generally, though not necessarily, includes those industries whose external economies or social returns are significant. (In this country, it has practically been limited to such industries.) Transport, gas, electricity and coal are good examples. Basic industries such as these produce far-reaching advantages throughout the economic system; so that calculations of returns on investments in them cannot be confined to their direct profits. It is even possible that a policy of low direct profits—as in the case of the Indian railways in the nineteenth century—is justified by the economic activity it stimulates all round. But we have to be cautious in following up such a policy, lest the calculation of indirect returns should become arbitrary and the limits to such a policy should tend to be unclear and sometimes dependent on objectionable or sectarian

[1] I. M. D. Little suggests, "if it is thought that interference is definitely required in order to make price more nearly equal to marginal cost, or for general social or military reasons, then this should be effected by means of taxation or subsidization." (*A Critique of Welfare Economics*, p. 210.)

[2] The Select Committee on Nationalized Industries commented on the National Coal Board's discussions with the Treasury on investments, as follows: "The discussions to this end are based on the average figure of the yields expected from the investments planned for the coming year; no details are given about the individual schemes that together make up that plan . . . it is purely an *average* figure that is discussed." (Report, para. 26.)

motives. It is easily possible to overestimate social returns in many cases—i.e., to overestimate the excess of the value of the product to the community over the price paid for it. The evaluation unfortunately is not amenable to accurate quantitative measurement.

(a) Among the considerations other than direct profit the most obvious are the requirements of defence and administration. In order to satisfy these requirements, it may be necessary to tackle questions of railway capacity and location, the location of certain heavy industrial units, etc., on other considerations than those of direct profit. If these requirements are accepted by Parliament and organized in the most efficient manner, there can be no objection to the allocations.

(b) The more common case of allocation on broad economic grounds arises where the planning technique adopted implies investments against profit criteria, at least in the short run. Such investments are common in the under-developed countries, as illustrated by the Second Five Year Plan of India. Railways, electricity and heavy industry account for about half of all the expenditures other than on social services. Their relative unprofitability, or low profitability, is due to two factors: firstly, there is no demand that pays for all the costs of the capacity set up, and no smaller capacity may be possible due to its indivisibility; secondly, discriminatory pricing is either difficult or not permitted. Nevertheless the Government may decide to introduce the investments in view of the external economies flowing from those industries, which—let us assume—are real and rigorously evaluated.

(c) Sometimes allocations are made to cater for the economic prosperity of certain regions. Examples are found in the nationalization of Pignone in Italy—an undertaking which was on the point of closure; and iron mines in north Sweden. The nearest example in the British context is the uneconomic coalmines that are not closed, in order to avoid local unemployment.

(d) At this stage we may refer to the Government's intentions in the field of income distribution. It is necessary for our discussion to specify the best pattern of income distribution. What is necessary to assume is that, firstly, the Government has a pattern in view and that, secondly, the managers of the nationalized industries neither know it by themselves nor are entitled to work towards it on their own responsibility. Under these conditions the Government may approach the question of resource allocation from the angle of promoting the distributive effects intended by it. The amount of allocation to an industry or in a region may be different on the test of its profitability than on the test of its distributive effects. If the allocation is decided because of the latter criterion, two important questions follow. Should the industries be instructed to adopt a policy of discriminatory prices analogous to cross-subsidization, so that the revenues of the industry cover its costs? Care must then be taken to see that the pricing structures do not neutralize the intended distributive effects. Or, should the industry be prevented from bringing about cross-subsidizations and the deficits met from subsidies? In the latter case, the responsibility for promoting the intended distributive effects falls on the taxpayer.

(e) Finally reference may be made to the policies of co-ordination applied to certain industries—e.g., transport and fuel. The case for an active external machinery of co-ordination, which subordinates the price system to external decisions, is not conclusive.[1] But all political decisions seeking a chosen order among industries prevent the capital mobilities that pure economic forces normally cause. Such decisions could be the most harmful in the long run to the evolution of the most economic inter-industry relationships.[2] Such a policy of co-ordination is indefensible, unless it is directly supported by any of the broad social issues cited above. It barely arises from a political evaluation of what the position of one industry and its consumers ought to be, *vis-à-vis* that of another. Co-ordination is likely to be a major interest under public enterprise, since there is a general anxiety, apart from the statutory need, to make every investment pay for itself; and the term (co-ordination) gains prominence in its financial sense. It is unfortunate that sufficient provision is not made for facilitating contraction of capacity in the necessary cases. To the extent that unnecessary capacities are maintained, there is what may be called a "constructive" over-allocation for some industries.

It is true that some of the above considerations must qualify the profitability criterion in determining allocations. That would ensure due regard being paid to the "social marginal productivity" of the investment—i.e., "the total net contribution of the marginal unit to national product, and not merely that portion of the contribution (or of its costs) which may accrue to the private investor".[3]

However, we are faced with the insuperable difficulty of im-

---

[1] For instance, the Ridley Committee observed that "the best pattern of fuel and power use will be promoted not by the direct intervention of the Government, but by the exercise of the consumer's free choice of his fuel services—provided that competition between the fuel industries is based on prices, tariffs, and terms of supply which closely correspond to the relevant costs of supply, and that the consumer is enabled to make an informed choice". (Para. 232, Report on the Committee on National Policy for the use of Fuel and Power Resources, 1952.)

[2] There are, however, several instances of desirable "co-operation between the fuel and power industries in production and distribution", as cited by the Ridley Committee. (*Op. cit.*, para. 226.)

[3] A. E. Khan, "Investment Criteria in Development Programs", *The Quarterly Journal of Economics*, 1951, p. 39.

measurability in following this concept in practice. External economies are a real phenomenon; yet they cannot be calculated with precision. H. B. Chenery gives the example of how, in the case of a railway meant to serve a new mining area, "the external effects can best be measured by taking the investment in the railroad as part of the total investment in the project."[1] In most cases the situation is far less simple. The effects of an investment are spread over several beneficiaries; and as the investing parties are not the same in all these cases the problem of allowing for the inter-industry benefits becomes acute as well as difficult.

The desirability of applying the social-cum-private returns test is qualified by the absence of helpful techniques of evaluating the social returns. Their assessment is likely to be influenced by arbitrary considerations; and evaluations suitable to the political climate of the times are likely to emerge. In view of the importance attached to the question of social returns, the Government may, however, revise the autonomous allocations to particular industries. But this should be followed by appropriate subsidies in order to compensate for the direct consequences on the industries concerned. The question, fundamentally, is whether some consumers, who can be made to pay, should bear the burden of the over-allocations, which presumably is not borne by the beneficiaries of such over-allocations; or whether the taxpayers should bear it as a social overhead. It would be logical to cover the deficits traceable to non-autonomous allocations from general taxation. There is no reason why certain consumers should pay for them or why the managers of the nationalized industry should have the power of deciding on what really is a "tax spread".

Where an allocation is made specifically on non-commercial grounds, it is desirable to keep the capital outlay separate from the rest of the capital of the industry and to consider that the Board is in charge of it on government account. In some cases it is difficult to decide to what extent a certain investment is commercial and to what extent it is non-commercial; and a non-commercial investment may become commercial after a time. These difficulties need not destroy the principle; and approximate divisions may be made. The result of the isolation is that the commercial working of the public enterprise is separately assessable from its non-commercial role. To give an example, a part of the Indian railway capital has always been treated as non-commercial, for it was invested for military purposes. Such a step would provide against the consumers of the industry bearing the taxpayer's responsibility.

---

[1] H. B. Chenery, "The Application of Investment Criteria", *The Quarterly Journal of Economics*, 1953, p. 76.

The argument may now be concluded. The acceptance of the profitability criterion does not make impossible allocations which are justified on the other grounds enumerated above. The only qualification is that the non-autonomous allocations should be followed by appropriate compensations from the Government for the consequences on the industry concerned. Apart from placing the burden rightly on the taxpayer, such compensations keep the public fully informed of the cost of the non-autonomous allocations. This procedure has the advantage of restricting investment decisions basically to the criterion of profitability, while adjustments are made on government initiative.

At this stage the principles distinguishing the normal budget allocations of the Government from the allocations among public enterprises may be mentioned. Most of the budget allocations are not characterized by the test of price or self-support, which is the primary mark of distinction of a public enterprise. Some of the allocations, e.g., those under the heads of justice, police and sanitation, are meant to provide certain basic services to the community. The budget allocations are chiefly decided on the basis of social and political evaluations. Though the demands under different heads are co-ordinated by the Cabinet, there is no common denominator to compare, for example, the end of a certain number of school buildings with the end of a certain number of hospitals. Education and health have different values, which lack a homogeneous measuring rod, unlike gas and electricity; and they are not easily substitutable either. The decisions are, therefore, the result of social evaluations and obvious value judgements. It is the amenability of the priced services and outputs to a common measure in terms of money that distinguishes commercial enterprise from most part of the purely governmental activities and, therefore, makes it not only possible but necessary to regulate different outputs on the price and profit criteria.

In certain fields of budget allocation the physical targets are fixed at government instance. For example, the number of hospital beds for which provision shall be made or the number of medical students for whom facilities of education shall be given or the number of houses to be built in a five-year period, is decided, often as a measure of political convenience.[1] A better example would be the defence needs of which the determining factor is nothing but the Government's evaluation of military needs. Parliamentary approval gives these the stamp of what the Government thinks is good for the people and the allocations would be made towards those ends. In the case of commercial enterprise, on the other hand, it is difficult for a

[1] For example, the Labour Party and the Conservative Party had very different targets of house-building, at the time of the General Election in 1951.

Government, other than a totalitarian Government, to decide for the consumers what products, and how much of each product, are good for them. To the extent that the Government desires to preserve the consumers' freedom of choice, the market forces should have a decisive force on the allocations and the allocations, by and large, tend to be autonomous.

Finally, over-allocations (by whatever standard), in other than the purely commercial fields, have the over-all effect of adding to some kind of social benefits, not necessarily in money terms. For example, a few more schools or hospitals make for better education or better health; more police may improve the safety of living; more armies may strengthen the country's defence. Resources being scarce, it is true that more of one involves less of another; but it is difficult to show which alternative is absolutely superior to another, except during an exigency like war when the highest priority is known to be the winning of the war. The analogy fails in most cases as we turn to commercial enterprise. Arbitrary policy allocations run counter to the consumers' expressed intentions of choice; and they may be denied a product they want and receive one they do not want.

It is in recognition of all these differences in the principles of allocation that some of the departmental commercial enterprises are generally provided with separate budgets and allowed to proceed upon commercial principles of allocation. The need to preserve the latter is particularly great with the corporation form of organization, for by hypothesis its working is to be free from political influence.

## SELF-FINANCING

THE question of self-financing amounts to that of permissible profits for the nationalized industries, for under the British Nationalization Acts profits are not surrendered to the Government but remain with the industries concerned. This amounts to a re-investment of one kind or another.

### 1. *The importance of self-financing*

The importance of self-financing is derived mainly from four considerations.

(a) Decisions on the extent of self-financing have an impact on the price level and may sometimes tempt the managers to practise price discrimination.

(b) Since funds are found from current prices, there may be a relaxation of the economic criterion of whether the investments will be profitable by themselves. This is all the more certain where the cost of capital is ignored in the computation of the costs of the new output.

(c) Self-financing involves the transfer of benefits from the present consumers to the future consumers and from one consumer group or region to another consumer group or region. The latter is a case of cross-subsidization described in the Appendix to Chapter IV.

(d) Self-financing presupposes profits, which are subject to the provisions of income tax and profits tax. So, as self-financing assumes importance, the tax payments to the general exchequer increase—an incidental benefit to the taxpayer.

There is a twofold difference between public and private enterprise on the question of self-financing. In the first place, the profits which private enterprise earns with a view to self-financing are presumably earned under conditions of competition. Where competition becomes so imperfect as to relieve the undertakings of even the fear of potential competition, the opportunity of monopoly control is always open to the public. The recent finding of the Monopolies and Restrictive Practices Commission that the British Oxygen Company's profits are excessive illustrates a public attitude which is bound to have gradual influence on the Company's profits policy. Nationalized industries have a high degree of monopoly power and operate (so far) under unclear and inadequate pricing rules, so that the practical or potential checks, which affect the extent of self-financing in private enterprise, are absent.[1] Secondly, it is doubtful whether the present consumer necessarily subsidizes the future consumer under the system of self-financing in private enterprise. The answer really depends on whether the re-investment is treated as a cost-less outlay in so far as the future consumer is concerned. The costs of output made available to the future consumer are likely to include a proper charge for the capital used. Thus the present consumer may yield the benefit, not to the future consumer, but to the owner of the undertaking. It is probable that the re-investment of profits is followed by an issue of bonus shares, which may prompt the undertaking to consider that the total recoverable costs have increased because of the additional dividend claims. Once again the owner benefits but the future consumer does not.[2] The question essentially involved in self-financing under private enterprise is one of permissible profits for the benefit of the owner of the undertaking—a quite different question from that under British nationalization.

### 2. Effects

Let us examine how the process of self-financing works out through the pricing system of the industry. Two cases may be distinguished: (i) where the undertaking keeps within its optimum limits of size and serves consumers in inseparable markets, and (ii) where the undertaking serves separable markets.

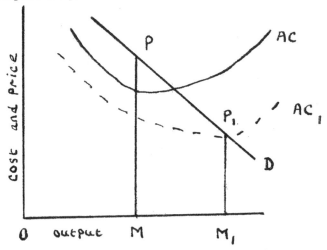

[1] The British Transport Commission is, of course, an exception.

[2] It is possible that in the short run the shareholders receive limited dividends because of the ploughing back of profits; but in the long run their position is greatly improved.

(i) Assume a uniform price of PM, which is so fixed as to earn some profit for re-investment. Consequent on re-investment, the cost curve is lowered to the position of $AC_1$ because (a) there is no addition to capital charges in the accountancy sense, though the opportunity costs of using capital increase, and (b) the outlays may have led to more economical techniques than before. If output expands as a result of the re-investment, the price must fall in order to sell more of the output than before. The lowest price possible is $P_1M_1$; and the actual price settles between $P_1M_1$ and PM, depending on the possibilities of further re-investment and expansion of output and the extent to which the undertaking wishes to cover it by self-financing. It is likely that such possibilities generally present themselves. In some cases at least re-investments take the shape of improving the quality of the existing output or of higher wage payments. The cost curve rises in these cases and profits are reduced.

The British Nationalization Acts do not permit of a transfer to the general exchequer of the profits of nationalized industries. Once the costs are fully recovered and adequate reserves are made not only for depreciation but also for interest charges, under the above assumptions of uniform price and inseparable markets, profits can only be either re-invested or liquidated through falling prices.

The effect of self-financing in this case is that the present prices are higher in order to make possible lower prices in the future. It is difficult to say whether, over time, the consumers are no worse off under the method of self-financing. For one thing the identity of the consumers may not be the same over a period. There are two important problems, further. Firstly, the policy of present high prices and future low prices may or may not agree with corresponding general economic conditions. Secondly, by recovering at present the costs of future use of factors employed, the undertaking will be at an advantage in future over its competitors. This is really an accounting advantage, which does not survive the test of real inputs involved.

(ii) Let us now turn to the more general case: markets are separable; price discrimination is practised; and the undertaking is large and supra-optimum in size. (Many of the public utilities like railways, electricity and gas come within this description.) Under these conditions self-financing can imply that some markets permanently pay high prices, that the profits resulting from those high prices are re-invested in some new market or region and that the prices in the new markets are possibly low. As a result cross-subsidization takes place permanently. This is a serious result of self-financing, which is apparently a method of securing funds for investment.

## 3. *Conclusion*

Self-financing is a widely practised method of investment finance. It implies that a certain proportion of investment is derived from the consumers, instead of all the funds being drawn from the investors. If this takes place over the non-nationalized industrial economy, it is proper that a similar tendency should develop inside the nationalized industrial sector. Otherwise the consumers of nationalized industries are favoured by a system of relatively low prices *vis-à-vis* the consumers of the other industries. As I. M. D. Little observes, "when it can be seen that a particular industry could make good profits without any apparent 'distortion' of output, then it seems manifestly wrong that it should throw the whole burden of finding the savings required for its own investment on the government or the rest of the community."[1]

A few qualifications may now be introduced. There are two aspects of the question of self-financing which it is desirable to distinguish. As a method of investment finance it may be justified on the above ground. But this is different from the question whether the new output in a different market should not be so costed as to include a capital charge. Though the capital charge is not paid out by the undertaking to any outside stockholder, it is a real cost in so far as the new consumer is concerned. (If it is desired, for any reason, that he should be subsidized, it amounts to an independent decision.) It is proper not to let the price of the new output be influenced by the accounting advantage of the absence of a capital charge but take up the question of a subsidized price separately. One advantage of this procedure is that each investment decision depends on the merits of its own profitability; and the mere fact that money is readily available does not relax the investment criteria.

The opportunities of self-financing are greater for the nationalized industries in view of their monopoly position. It is possible for many of them—e.g., the National Coal Board—if given the freedom to maximize profits, to find a large proportion of their investment funds internally. It is, therefore, necessary, as an element of monopoly control, to specify the permissible profits for each nationalized industry, in broad terms. (At present a limit to the amount that can be transferred to the reserves is specified only in the case of the gas industry.)[2] The extent of self-financing permitted must, of course, bear some relation to the conditions prevailing elsewhere in the industrial economy.

---

[1] I. M. D. Little, *op. cit.*, p. 215.
[2] Section 46 (2), Gas Act, 1948.

The Herbert Committee in fact came to the conclusion that the electricity industry ought not to attempt at self-financing once it has met "its costs, maintained its capacity intact and secured a modest contribution to reserves". They put the last one at one per cent on capital and observed, "in our opinion publicly-owned electricity undertakings should not go beyond the limits described" above.[1]

Lastly, self-financing ought not to be so employed as to imply gross cross-subsidization. Where the industry is empowered to use its aggregate profit for re-investment anywhere in the system, it is probable that the profitable parts of it subsidize the development of the unprofitable ones and for all time. Such inter-transfers of funds ought not to be automatic.

In conclusion, we may note the actual position of the nationalized industries in respect of self-financing. Careful examination of the profits earned by them up-to-date does not indicate that much self-financing has been undertaken by them. The fact seems to be that the prices have been kept too low to serve this purpose. The reason is partly political and partly linked with the Government's policy of price freeze. It is desirable to let the industries operate at prices that permit of self-financing within specified limits and subject to the above qualifications.

There is possibly a clash of interests on the question of self-financing. There is the economic justification for it, within limits, on the one side; and on the other, there are political difficulties in the way of permitting high prices and high profits. After all, the present consumers are a force to reckon with: they are the voters.

[1] Report of the Committee of Inquiry into the Electricity Supply Industry, 1956, paras. 341, 343.

For Product Safety Concerns and Information please contact our EU
representative GPSR@taylorandfrancis.com Taylor & Francis Verlag GmbH,
Kaufingerstraße 24, 80331 München, Germany

Printed and bound by CPI Group (UK) Ltd, Croydon, CR0 4YY
08/05/2025
01864366-0004